GHOSTS, LEGENDS and LORE of WALES

P.H. J...

GW00642648

Copyright © The Old Orchard Press
Printed by The Burlington Press (Cambridge) Ltd, Foxton, Cambridge.
ISBN 1 870301 05 6

£3.50

GHOSTS, LEGENDS and LORE of WALES

CONTENTS

ILLUSTRATIONS

Introduction

Wales is a land soaked in legend. Oft-told bardic tales relate the deeds of valiant heroes, beautiful maidens and treacherous villains. The landscape bears the names of warlords, saints and wizards, real and mythical, from centuries long ago while folklore's long memory preserves stories of fairy enchantment, giants, monsters and hidden treasure.

Many localities claim to have the secret cave where King Arthur, the shadowy Dark Ages warrior and hero of medieval romance, lies sleeping with his knights awaiting the call to return when danger threatens to overwhelm the land of the Britons. Merlin, the magician and prophet, endures timeless slumber, held by the bonds of an enchantress. The names of Llywelyn and Dafydd, the sometimes ally, sometimes enemy brother-princes of Gwynedd, are carried by two of the highest Snowdonian peaks. The deeds and eventual disappearance of Owain Glyndwr, the patriot prince whose rebellion briefly threw off English rule, became the stuff of later legend and lore.

Fairy folk, the diminutive pagan guardians of supernatural powers who beguile mere mortals with their music and dance, are prominent in the traditional tales. Stories tell of their dread of iron and repugnance of human greed and deceit – reprehensible yet constant traits which are echoed in tales of beasts and fairy maidens who endowed prosperity upon their mortal human masters and partners until avarice and selfishness were punished by a swift return to poverty. Often it was prophesied that hoards of gold could only be discovered by a pauper youth or maiden (in folklore riches should be the reward of innocence and gentleness, not the looted spoils of armed invading warlords). Is not the crime of a conqueror at the head of an army the same as that of a bandit merely magnified ten-thousandfold? In legend the 'heroic' kings, princes and warriors are often portrayed as parasitic gorgers of meat and drink whose authority was imposed by the sword. And in many a ghostly tale the restless spirit manifests itself only to right a wrong.

Chronicler-priests like Gerald of Wales and Geoffrey of Monmouth (the latter famous for his fanciful history of Britain) recorded the miracles performed by the saints – the men and women, hermits and missionaries who fostered and spread the Christian faith among the Britons while heathen English invaders continued their idolatrous reverence to the gods of their Continental ancestors. Water, that source and sustainer of life, features prominently in many an ancient tale, and the wells of the saints where converts were baptised became renowned for their supposed ability to cure all sorts of ills and ailments. Wizardry, valour and vengeance; cupidity, brutality and pride; love, lust, treachery, betrayal and greed, are some of the woven strands of the myths and legends of Wales, a land whose emblem is a fiery red dragon.

Heroes, heroines, villains and wizards of myth and history

Magic spells, bloody murder, treachery, loyalty, wickedness and lust are a few of the attributes of legendary tales of every age and every region, and sometimes the acts of historical characters (or at least the folklore memory of them and their deeds) match the fabulous tales of kings and warriors, battles and betrayals. Many a story associated with the lakes, mountains and islands of Wales come from the Mabinogion, a collection of tales based on 14th century Welsh manuscripts. The stories themselves, however, are much older and preserve tales of pagan Celtic times which had been transmitted orally down the centuries. Among the cast of characters are wizards and warlords, kings and princes, giants, dwarfs and a dazzling parade of beautiful maidens, as well as that most famous hero of British legend, Arthur. They inhabit a violent, thuggish world where men have more brawn than brain, spending their days eating, drinking, brawling, hunting, and lustfully pursuing ladies. Macho pride rules; insults and loss of face are rancorously avenged. The women are either desirable beauties or ugly crones. The good looking ones are there to satisfy all male desires, to be fought over and rescued, and to provide the motives for blood-letting battles and decapitation.

Pwyll, Prince of Dyfed, was a brave and honourable man who held his court at Narberth, and one day when he had not much to do he went for a walk to the top of a nearby magical mound – those who sat on the top could not leave without receiving a wound or witnessing a wonder. Pwyll was lucky, he saw a beautiful woman riding a white horse. Rhiannon was her name and she told Pwyll, who fell in love with her there and then, that she was being forced to marry against her will and that the only man she really wanted to wed was Pwyll himself. To solve the problem, they decided to get married and the wedding feast was proving to be a great success when Pwyll, who was not the brighter half of the partnership, ruined everything. A stranger came striding into the hall and craved a boon. "Anything you like," said Pwyll, not knowing that the interloper was the man to whom Rhiannon had been pledged.

Having obtained the prince's promise in the presence of witnesses, the unwelcome guest demanded Rhiannon for himself. Fortunately Rhiannon, who had an intellect sharper than any of the men, had a plan to get them out of the mess created by Pwyll's stupidity. When Rhiannon's father laid on a wedding feast in honour of the new bridegroom-to-be, Pwyll came marching into the hall disguised as a beggar and asked his rival to grant him the favour of filling his bag with food. Plate after plate of meat was tipped into the magic hold-all provided by Rhiannon and when the unloved guest of honour protested about the way his wedding victuals were vanishing from the tables, Pwyll told him it would stop if he put his feet in the bag. The foolish man obliged, Pwyll whipped the bag shut, trapping his rival inside, and then blew his horn to summon his

The Rock of Harlech with its medieval castle – here a king spied a fleet and Branwen's troubles began.

warriors who had been hiding in the orchard. As they came in they each gave the bag a kick until the battered suitor agreed to give up his claim.

Pwyll and Rhiannon had a son but the child had been in the world only a few hours when he disappeared. The six babysitters who had neglected their charge by dozing during the night, awoke to find a crisis, and as the consequences of mislaying a prince were too dreadful to contemplate, they concocted a plot whereby it appeared that Rhiannon had murdered her infant. That same night, in another part of the realm, a man was in his stable when a huge claw came through the window, grabbing at a new-born colt. He drew his sword, chopped off the demonic arm and during the resulting commotion discovered an infant on his doorstep. Eventually it was realised that the foundling was Pwyll's son and, to great rejoicing, the boy, Pryderi, was restored to his parents and Rhiannon's punishment of carrying every visitor on her back came to an end.

Destiny decreed that no happy ending awaited Branwen after marriage to a king. Her tale of woe began the day her brother, King Bran, was sitting on the rock of Harlech and saw the fleet of Matholwych of Ireland nearing the coast. He had made the voyage hoping to make an alliance with Bran by marrying the King of Britain's sister. The kings and their courtiers went to the royal palace at Aberffraw to celebrate the wedding but the happy occasion was clouded by Bran's trouble-making half-brother who insulted the touchy Irish monarch by maiming his horses. Bran atoned for the shame by giving his new brother-in-law a magic cauldron, once the property of giants, which had the useful quality of being able to restore dead warriors to life. So the breach was healed, Branwen sailed off to Ireland with her new husband and in due time she was delivered of a son. Unfortunately the insult rankled with the proud Irish and Matholwych was persuaded to put an embargo on trade, cut the ferry links and lock up foreigners. They even took it out on poor Branwen who was banished to the kitchens where daily she got a clout around the ears from the court butcher. But Branwen was a resourceful maid – she wrote a letter about her sufferings and despatched it to her brother by bird.

Bran mobilised his army and invaded Ireland – the coastguards reported seeing a mountain and a forest coming across the sea; what they did espy was Bran, a true giant of a man, towing his fleet. Peace talks started – Matholwych was to abdicate in favour of his son – and there it might have ended but for Bran's villainous half-brother who displayed the unpleasant side of his character by picking up the child and throwing him on the fire. Swords were drawn and battle ensued. The Irish got out their 'secret weapon', the magic cooking pot, into which they tossed the corpses of their dead to make good their losses. The man whose acts had been the cause of so much strife put a stop to the flow of reinforcements by jumping in among the bodies and exploding the cauldron by bursting his heart. When the battle ended only Bran, who had been wounded by a poisoned spear, and seven of his warriors were left alive. Bran ordered his men to chop off his head and bury it in London (on the site of the

Tower of London) facing France because no invader would land on British soil as long as his head was hidden there. When the little band reached Anglesey Branwen died of despair and a broken heart and was buried at Bedd Branwen near Llanbabo. The guardians of the king's head journeyed to Harlech where they passed seven years feasting and listening to the spellbinding song of Rhiannon's birds before going off to London to carry out their king's last wish.

Two survivors of the Irish wars were Pryderi, Pwyll's lost-and-found son, and Bran's brother, Manawyddan, who is the hero of another tale of magic and wizardry. Manawyddan's estates had been usurped while he was campaigning in Ireland so Pryderi persuaded him to go with him to Dyfed and there the landless veteran fell in love with and married Pryderi's widowed mother, Rhiannon, who was still a comely creature. They feasted and enjoyed life at Narberth until the fateful day a terrible storm and mist enveloped the land. When the sky cleared the land was deserted; servants and peasants, cattle and goats, houses and cottages had all vanished. Pryderi and Manawyddan provided for themselves and their wives by hunting across the forsaken land but further calamity was in store. Pryderi came across a deserted castle with a golden fountain standing where he had never seen one before, but his delight turned to helpless rage because as soon as he touched the fountain he was struck dumb and stuck to the spot. Along came Rhiannon and she too was rendered speechless and rooted when she touched the fountain. Then, with a crash of thunder, mother, son and magic castle vanished.

Manawyddan, alone but for Pryderi's disconsolate wife, turned his back on the accursed land to earn his living as a shoemaker in Hereford. The trouble was that he was exceptionally good at cobbling, cornering the market for luxury footwear. When angry competitors plotted to end his success with a knife in his back, he packed his bags, bought some seed-corn and returned to Narberth where he and Pryderi's wife settled down to life on a farm. He proved to be as good a farmer as he was a cordwainer, and when harvest time came he had three fields of top-quality wheat ready for the scythe. He prepared to reap the first two fields but during the night every ear of grain vanished and he was left with a couple of crofts of stripped stalks. Manawyddan kept a vigil over the remnant of his crop and at midnight a plague of mice invaded the wheatfield. Before he could intervene every wheat ear had been carried away although he did manage to get his hands on one of the pests and imprison it in an old glove. He decided to make an example of the captured four-legged felon and on top of the mysterious mound at Narberth he began building a mouse-sized gallows. The execution was interrupted by a tattily clad cleric who offered a pound for the condemned mouse's release, an offer which was rejected. Then appeared a well-dressed priest on a horse who raised the bounty to three pounds but again Manawyddan refused. As he was tightening the string noose around the rodent's neck along came a rich bishop with retinue of servants and loaded packhorses who upped the rescue price to include

The tumbling waters of Afon Cynfal where a legendary hero vengefully speared his unfaithful wife's lover.

cash and baggage-train. Then, due to Manawyddan's insistence, the cause of all the calamities was revealed. It was no bishop who was pleading for the mouse's reprieve but a wizard who had laid a curse on the land in revenge for the bag-trapping trick Pwyll had pulled on the man who had wanted to marry Rhiannon. It was the magician who had caused Pryderi and his mother to vanish stuck to a fountain, and it was he who had turned his kinfolk and servants into mice to strip the wheatfields; a plan which had backfired when Manawyddan had captured the wizard's less than nimble wife. The price of her release was an end to the feud, the return of Pryderi and Rhiannon, and the lifting of the curse to restore Dyfed to being a fruitful and populous land.

Prince Pryderi's adventurous life came to an end in a duel with another wizard. Gwydion had used his spells to steal a prize herd of swine and when Pryderi's army chased the rustlers there was a battle with Math and the men of Gwynedd. Pryderi and his war-band were pursued through the mountains and along the coast till they came to Maentwrog where it was agreed that the matter should be settled by single combat between Pryderi and the magician. Watched by the two armies, Gwydion used his wizardry to slay the Prince of Dyfed. Gwydion then got involved in further magical escapades in which he fashioned a woman, Blodeuedd, out of wild flowers as a wife for Lleu Llaw Gyffes. She proved to be unfaithful and plotted with her lover to eliminate Lleu but the problem was that he was virtually spear-proof. His 'Achilles heel' was that he could only be slain when bathing in a river while balanced on the back of a goat. Blodeuedd turned on her feminine charm, wheedled the secret out of her husband and arranged to have a goat handy when he went to the river for his bath. The lover waited for the moment of vulnerability, let fly and found his mark – Lleu was transformed into a rotting eagle.

Gwydion used his magic to turn Lleu back into a man and then, with an army at their command, they marched on Tomen-y-Mur, Lleu's castle, where the lovers were enjoying themselves. Blodeuedd saw them coming and headed for the hills with her court-maidens who blundered into a lake, now known as Llyn Morwynion (lake of the maidens), and drowned. Gwydion cast a magic spell which turned Blodeuedd into an owl and that left the lover to be dealt with. Lleu forced his victim to stand where he himself had taken his near-fatal bath and despatched him with a spear thrust. The spot where he gained his revenge is marked, so they say, by a stone with a hole the size of a spear shaft beside the river Cynfal.

King Arthur makes his appearance in the Mabinogion in a series of quests and daring deeds. It was thanks to Arthur and his knights that Culhwch managed to accomplish all the tasks necessary to win Olwen as his bride – a happy conclusion for all except her father who had his head chopped off. Olwen was the only woman in the world for Culhwch and she was the daughter of a man-mangling giant (the brutish, bloodthirsty giants of the Mabinogion had a propensity for producing desirable daughters). Culhwch took his father's advice and rode off with his silver spears and golden sword to cousin Arthur's court to seek help. Arthur was not one to turn down the chance of excitement and he recruited a band of adventurers including a guide who never got lost, a man who could speak every language and a magician who could make them invisible. When they eventually arrived at the giant's castle there was no warm welcome awaiting them – the ogre threw poisoned spears at them. They countered this display of inhospitality by catching the missiles and throwing them back, one lodging in the big fellow's eyeball which brought water to his eyes and gave him a nasty headache. Blonde Olwen, in whose dainty footsteps flowers appeared, was a most beautiful creature and well worth winning whatever the dangers. Her giant father, however, was not going to make the wooing easy and he listed forty nigh impossible tasks to be accomplished before Culhwch could make her his bride.

The giant's list of demands required the suitor to clear a forest and plough and sow the land for food for the wedding feast, get a magic harp and the birds of Rhiannon to entertain the guests, obtain some witch's blood in a bottle and, most perilous of all, get comb and scissors to smarten up the giant's beard. The problem with the latter utensils was that they were affixed to the head of a monstrous wild boar. The hunt ranged far and wide from Ireland to Wales and Cornwall. The beastly boar (the reincarnation of a wicked king) killed many of Arthur's men and ancient stones on Mynydd Preseli are said to mark some of the victims' graves, and other mountain-top boulders have, if you look closely, the paw imprint of Arthur's favourite hunting hound. With the aid of Arthur and his warriors, and after many bloody adventures, all the tasks were successfully completed and Culhwch returned to the giant's castle to claim his bride. He ruled the giant's dominion from the stronghold which was decorated with the ogre's head stuck on a stake.

In another tale King Arthur relaxes at his court at Caerleon, and having no giants to kill or quests to pursue that day he decides to take a nap while some of his knights amuse themselves by eating, drinking and telling of their daring deeds. Cynon begins by relating how, when he was overflowing with youthful confidence, he went in search of adventure and came across a castle inhabited by two dozen beauties. The least lovely of them, said Cynon, outshone even Arthur's wife – perhaps it was just as well the king was snoozing and Guinevere was busy with her needlework when he dropped in this extra detail. Then he met a one-legged black cyclops, discovered a magic fountain, survived a violent storm and was defeated by a fearsome black knight who stole his horse.

Among the listeners to Cynon's story was Owain, one of Arthur's most loyal knights, and he decides to go in search of the fountain and the black knight. The real Owain was son of Urien of Rheged, a Celtic kingdom covering Cumbria, and, traditionally, he was a grandson of 'old King Coel'. In later Arthurian romance he is slain, his head cleft to the teeth, by a two-handed sword blow by wicked cousin Mordred. The rest of the tale entitled 'The Lady of the Fountain' tells of Owain's hair-raising scrapes which end in marriage to the lady of the title. His journey takes him to the edge of the world where he enjoys the ministrations of 24 lovelies, meets the one-eyed giant, discovers the magic fountain, and chases the guardian knight whose head he had split open. His pursuit of the dying warrior led to a city but Owain ran into trouble when the portcullis came thundering down and cut his horse in half. Trapped with angry townsmen mustering to avenge their master's death, Owain had a stroke of luck. A blonde took a fancy to him and gave him a magic ring which made him invisible so that all the avengers found was half a horse. With the subtle help of his rescuer Owain became the ruler of the land by marrying the countess he had so recently widowed and he made a nice profit on the side as the new guardian of the fountain by up-ending and ransoming any knights who came that way.

The tales of Peredur and Gereint, two more of Arthur's invincible warriors, are full of jousts, giant-killings and beautiful maidens. A Peredur who ruled in northern England was killed by Saxons in the late sixth century and Gereint is the name of British kings of Devon and Cornwall who clashed with the invaders. The Gereint of Welsh legend answers a summons to return to Cornwall to defend his father's lands and among the knights who rode with him was Peredur. The seventh son of a family whose menfolk had been killed in battle, Peredur (the Percival of later tales) enjoyed a non-martial childhood far from the clash of swords and braggart talk of warriors but all chance of him leading a pacific life ended when he saw some knights riding by and, with imagination fired, he decided to seek adventure. His mother, perceiving that he was determined to make a name for himself, gave her blessing, telling him to rescue maidens in distress, say his prayers regularly and make love whene'er he fancied. So Peredur set off for King Arthur's court on a scraggy nag clutching home-made weapons and it was not long before he notched his first kill. A bumptious knight who had tipped wine over Queen Guinevere's bosom was first to fall to Peredur's spear and the victory provided him with armour and warhorse. Properly equipped, Peredur rode off in search of more adventures and sent a stream of unhorsed knights back to Arthur's court to tell of his skill at arms.

Gereint's story, packed with episodes of murderous mayhem, has a thread of human emotional conflict and frailty which gives the two main characters some credibility. Gereint was a man who loved to gain renown in tournaments but when he marries the fair Enid he becomes a new man. He turns his back on the 'manly' life of court carousals, bloodsports and jousts in favour of passing most of his time with his wife. Tongues wag and when Enid blames herself for her husband's fading warrior reputation he imputes false motives for her concern. Unfounded suspicion blinds him to her true love even when she warns of danger and ambush. A bloody encounter with three club-carrying giants opens Gereint's unhealed wounds and as he lingers close to death Enid becomes the object of unwanted attentions by a lustful nobleman. This pesky lord tries to get her to slip into something simple as he plies her

Caernarfon – a Roman emperor dreamed of its mighty castle and then came in search of a beautiful bride.

with drink but when gentle seduction fails he becomes violent and Enid's screams rouse Gereint from melancholic decline. Realising his foolishness, he picks up his sword, hastens to the rescue of his true love and slices the molester in half. Gereint then mounts his horse, lifts Enid up in front of him and off they ride together to live happily ever after.

The story of the brothers Lludd and Llefelys tells how Britain was rid of three plaguey nuisances. Lludd, so the tale claims, was the king who ringed London, the city named after him, with strong walls. Llefelys gained a kingdom of his own by marrying a young Queen of France and while he was wisely ruling that land, Lludd's realm was smitten by three dire calamities. A sharp-eared race of invaders poured in and they could overhear every conversation so all poor Lludd's plans to get rid of them came to nothing. Then there was a terrible scream which caused women to miscarry, turned strong men into weaklings and made the land a desert. The third disaster was a giant who burgled the king's pantry in the middle of the night leaving only crumbs for the royal breakfast. Lludd sailed to France for brotherly advice which was whispered down a tube to prevent any eavesdropping. Lludd hastened home, called a meeting and when all were gathered together he sprayed the assembly with a concoction which killed off the invaders but left his own people unharmed. The awful scream was caused by two fighting dragons and to catch them Lludd dug a hole at the centre of his kingdom – his surveyors made Oxford the place – and then trapped them in a big bowl of sweet wine. As soon as the dreadful dragons drank the wine and dozed off they were packed off to Dinas Emrys in Snowdonia and locked away in a cave where, in another legend, their battles gave King Vortigern problems until Merlin came along. To catch the food-snatcher King Lludd laid on a great feast and sat up all night taking cold baths when he felt sleepy. In the dark hours a giant appeared with a tuck box, Lludd won the ensuing swordfight, and the mystery of the vanishing victuals was solved.

Two other Mabinogion tales tell of dreams. Rhonabwy, a soldier of Powys, has his dream when billeted in a filthy, dung-ridden, and flea-infested hovel. In his vision of the Arthurian golden age he meets famous men from the past. He is transported to Arthur's camp beside the Severn and encounters the man whose lies caused the epoch-ending Battle of Camlan in which Arthur was mortally wounded, Elphin from the flooded lands, the noble knight Owain, the boastful Cei (Kay) whose stronghold was, according to local tradition, the Roman camp at Caergai near Bala, and ugly-eared March the slayer of barbers. March (Welsh for horse) whose home was Castellmarch near Abersoch, was born with horse's ears, a misfortune which he tried to hide by wearing hats. But he could not keep his secret from barbers so when his hair had been trimmed he silenced the witnesses and dumped the corpses in a bog. One day a young musician went to the marsh in search of a reed to fashion into a pipe and when he stood up to play at March's feast all that came out was a mocking voice proclaiming "March has got horse ears, March has got horse ears!" March tried to get a less embarrassing tune out of the instrument but all his puff produced was "March has got horse ears!" Acknowledging that his secret was out, March spared the piper and from then on hairdressers ceased to fear appointments at Castellmarch.

Magnus Maximus, a Spanish soldier who set himself up as ruler of half the Roman Empire, was a popular man in late fourth century Britain. He defeated the Picts and Scots and then took his troops to Gaul where he killed the Emperor Gratian, but his ambition was boundless and he died fighting in Italy. Magnus made such an impression that down the centuries the bards told and retold his story in 'The Dream of Macsen Wledig'. In the tale Macsen, who had been hunting near Rome, took an afternoon nap and dreamed of sailing across the sea to Britain, the loveliest isle in the world, where, after more travels, he came to a castle wherein sat the most beautiful woman he had ever seen. Unfortunately, he had just put his arms around this alluring maiden when he awoke. Men were despatched to find the lady of his dreams and eventually they came to Caernarfon where they found everything – castle, lovely lady, gold and jewels – just as Macsen had described. Elen was stunned when the strangers offered to make her Empress of Rome so she told them to tell their master to come and get her himself. When he got the news Macsen hurried to Wales, swept the lady off her golden throne and made her his wife. A big construction programme followed with his raising strongholds at Caernarfon, Caerleon and Carmarthen and her overseeing the building of a network of roads, including Sarn Helen, the main Roman road of western Wales which linked Caer Moridunum (Carmarthen) and Caerhun in the Conwy valley. Meanwhile Rome had been seized by a usurper so Macsen laid siege to the Eternal City. Month after month the battle dragged on until Elen's crafty brothers turned up with reinforcements and stormed the walls while everyone else was having a break for lunch. The historical Elen was later revered as St Helen of Caernarfon and it is said that her son, Publicius, was the Peblig who gave his name to a church of ancient foundation at Llanbeblig. Pen-y-gaer near Caerhun, a hillfort with unusual defences of pointed stones, is linked by tradition with the road-building 'Empress of Rome' (it was once known as Caer Elen). Caernarfon also has a traditional claim to being the birthplace of Constantine the Great, the first Christian emperor of Rome. Geoffrey of Monmouth's erratic history says that Constantine's mother, another Helen who became a saint, was the daughter of 'old King Coel' and it is said that in later life she forsook her pagan ways, did many good works and went to Jerusalem where she discovered the True Cross on which Christ was crucified.

An anti-Roman warrior who entered Welsh mythology was Caratacus, warlord of the Catuvellauni of lowland Britain. His father was Cunobelinus (Shakespeare's Cymbeline) and his ancestor Cassivellaunus, who had opposed Julius Caesar's invasion in 54 BC, went into legend as the owner of a magic cloak which made him usefully invisible in battle. Caratacus (Caradog) fought the Romans for eight years, latterly leading the Celtic warriors of Wales, and legend says his final stand was below the hillfort of Caer Caradoc near Clun, although a site more favoured by historians is Cefn Carnedd hillfort near Caersws. A few miles north, near Church Stretton, is another Caer Caradoc and a third overlooks Cerrigidrudion where, folk memory claims, the fugitive Caratacus was clapped into irons by the pro-Roman Queen Cartimandua and handed over to his enemies.

While Magnus, the man who had stripped the country's defences in his pursuit of glory, gets a 'good press' from the storytellers, Vortigern, who ruled in the mid-fifth century, is portrayed as a tyrannical villain whose policies were a disaster for the Celtic people of Britain. Vortigern hired Saxon mercenaries like Hengist and Horsa but when there were problems over pay these invited allies became conquering invaders and the story of England began. Legend links Vortigern with several places, notably Dinas Emrys where plans to build a castle were frustrated by the dragons King Lludd had put there. When the builders' work kept vanishing Vortigern consulted his magicians and they told him that he was wasting his time until the blood of a boy who had no human father was mixed with the mortar. Messengers were sent to find such an unlikely child and in Carmarthen they heard a lad being taunted about his unknown father. So, with Merlin appearing to be a good candidate to provide the vital bonding agent, he and his mother, a king's daughter, were packed off to Snowdonia. Merlin's mother, a ravished nun, could not throw much light on the identity of the 'man' who had fathered the young prodigy because whoever it was had been invisible when he made love to her. Vortigern thought her story was stretching credibility beyond reasonable bounds so he sought expert opinon and was told that it was just the sort of thing demons who lived near the moon got up to. When Merlin was told that the king was literally after his blood he set about proving expert opinion was not always to be trusted. "You can't build a castle on top of dragons!" he told Vortigern who ordered further excavation which, as Merlin had predicted, revealed a pair of fire-breathing battling beasts. The two dragons, one red and one white, represented the warring Britons and Saxons said Merlin, who then launched into a catalogue of calamitous prophecies before adding that Vortigern's own horoscope looked anything but rosy. Legend says that Vortigern met his end in Nant Gwrtheyrn (Vortigern's valley) near Llithfaen below Yr Eifl, on one peak of which is the ancient hillfort of Tre'r Ceiri (town of giants). Merlin's home town of Carmarthen has long harboured the tradition that should the wizard's old oak topple then disaster will strike the town.

It was Geoffrey of Monmouth who changed the course of Arthurian legend. The hunting, questing and feasting warlord of the Mabinogion was thrust onto the wider European stage. Arthur was made to hold court in Paris, fight Romans, conquer Norway, Ireland, Iceland and Gaul, and even conceive the idea of making the whole continent his kingdom. But before all these far-flung adventures came to pass it had been due to Merlin's wizardry with potions that this British superman came into the world. King Uther was going wild with uncontrolled desire for Ygerna, wife of the Duke of Cornwall, and to satisfy the king's passion Merlin turned him into the living likeness of her husband. The Arthur of legend had a lot of trouble with giants. He slayed them from Mont St Michel off Brittany to Snowdon where he disposed of Retho, an ogre whose hobby was collecting his victims' beards to make a fur coat. Another Snowdonian giant gave his name to Cadair Ifan Goch, the mount on which he sat while he washed his feet in the river Conwy. Other old tales tell of a giant who liked to eat a Christian each day but out of grudging respect for the sabbath ate two on Saturdays and slept on Sundays. Many places claim that Arthur passed their way during his adventures. Ancient megaliths and stones from Gower to Anglesey are associated with him and they are explained as pebbles which got in his shoes or the tombs of his victims. Parc le Breos is a prehistoric tomb in Gower which produced several human skeletons when excavated, although folklore claimed it was a giant's grave. Maen Ceti near Llanrhidian was also called Arthur's Stone and local tradition has it that lovelorn young ladies who crawled around it under a full moon could conjure up the object of their desire if his heart was true.

On Mynydd Preseli where Arthur and his warriors chased a fearsome boar, there are a monster's grave (Bedd-yr-Afanc), stones marking the graves of Arthur's sons killed in the hunt (Carreg Meibion Arthur) and even the grave of the king himself (Bedd Arthur). Also in Dyfed is the hillfort of Craig Gwrtheyrn (Vortigern's rock) which tradition claims to be another of that king's strongholds. The slipped capstone of Coeten Arthur (Arthur's quoit, also called Cors-y-Gedol) in Dyffryn Ardudwy is another troublesome stone thrown from Arthur's shoe, and another of his 'quoits' is near Llanystumdwy. Just over the Powys border near Dorstone is Arthur's Stone which tradition says is where another victim of Arthur's giant-killing acts lies buried. A chronicler long ago recorded another burial mound in the region which was the grave of Anir, Arthur's son, but it could not be measured accurately because it changed shape.

Snowdonia has many enduring legends of Arthur. Bwlch-y-saethau (pass of the arrows) is where he was mortally wounded and nearby Llyn Llydaw is another watery hiding place of the sword Excalibur (the Arthur of Welsh legend had a sword called Caliburn). His kitchen well was near Llanberis and in the mountains west of the Roman fort of Caerhun, near the burial chamber of Maen-y-Bardd (the bard's stone), are relics of another of Arthur's giant-killings, standing stones called Ffon-y-cawr (the giant's staff) and Picell Arthur (Arthur's spear). And somewhere amid the peaks Arthur and his knights are slumbering, awaiting the call to return. They sleep with their treasure and tales of attempts to find Arthur's golden hoard abound. One such story, in many ways similar to that of the Pedlar of Swaffham, tells of a lad who went in search of his fortune and met a stranger on London Bridge. Together they returned to the grove where the young man had cut his hazelwood staff and there they uncovered a secret passage. They entered a huge

Devil's Bridge where three bridges span the Mynach and a cunning countrywoman outwitted the Devil.

cave in which Arthur and his knights were sleeping with their weapons and treasure. Nearby hung a bell which, the stranger cautioned, must not be tolled but the young man stumbled against it as he carried off an armful of gold. "Has the hour come?" demanded the awakening Arthur. "Nay, you must sleep more," replied the stranger. The young man was profligate with his gold and when he returned to replenish his purse he accidentally rang the bell again. The warriors stirred and reached for their swords. "Has the hour come?" Arthur called. The unfortunate gold-gatherer stammered and stuttered but failed to remember the tranquilising phrase. He emerged into the daylight empty-handed, black and blue, and never again did he find the cave of gold.

Merlin, who some say sleeps near Carmarthen while others claim that he rests on Bardsey Island or near Dynevor's old castle, foretold the tribulations of the Britons, and legend has it that Arthur brought many troubles upon himself by digging up Bran's head in London. While writers of Arthur's life say that he had things his own way in his battles with giants and serpents, chroniclers say he was given lessons in humility when he got bossy with the saints. When he crossed St Padarn, founder of a monastery at Llanbadarn Fawr, he was swallowed by the earth up to his chin and there he stayed until he repented. The ruined abbey of Strata Florida (Ystrad Fflur or valley of flowers) is linked to the most famous of Arthurian adventures, the Quest for the Holy Grail. Legend claims that the cup used at the Last Supper was brought to Glastonbury by Joseph of Arimathea and that the holy relic was passed on to the Cistercian monks of Strata Florida, one of the most famous monastic houses of medieval Wales and a burial place for many medieval Welsh princes. When greedy Henry VIII closed the monasteries the wooden cup was smuggled away to Nanteos for safe keeping. It is said that it was while staying in the mansion that Richard Wagner's imagination was fired, perhaps by the cup, to compose his version of the quest story, the opera 'Parsifal'.

The monks of Strata Florida bequeathed other local lore amid the rivers and mountains of northern Dyfed. The monks who were renowned for their sheep-herding expertise, spanned the rushing waters of Afon Mynach (Monks' river) with a little bridge which became known as Pont-y-gwrdrwg, Bridge of the Evil One. Long ago, the story goes, there lived on one side of the river an old country woman, Marged, who grazed her old cow on the far bank. She found wading across to bring the beast home for milking a troublesome and dampening chore and one day she was paddling through the water when she was accosted by a monk (it was the Devil in disguise) who offered to build her a bridge on condition that he could have the soul of the first creature to cross. The grandam readily agreed gratefully to the plan and the Evil One, rubbing his hands in expectation, got to work. When it was finished Marged, who was no rustic simpleton, tossed a crust across and her dog was first to test the new construction and go to hell. The Mynach, renowned for its series of waterfalls which include one cascade of more than 100 feet, joins the

Rheidol at Devil's Bridge and tradition says that a cave near one of the falls was the hideout of a sinister trio of two brothers and a sister who robbed and murdered travellers. A mile upstream of the Rheidol's own cataracts is an iron bridge built by a later man of the Church – Parson's Bridge which leads to Ysbyty Cynfyn where the monks had a wayside hospice (ysbyty). The church stands within a circular churchyard, a feature of Celtic early Christian foundations not uncommon in Wales, and older still are the stones which remain from the original pagan circle of menhirs. Another near-intact ancient circle of stones lies across Parson's Bridge on the slopes of Bryn Bras.

Bwlch y Groes (Pass of the Cross) between Bala and Mallwyd – 'one of the most terrible in North Wales' according to the 18th century travel writer, Thomas Pennant – was an area to be avoided in the mid-16th century. It was the haunt of murderous brigands known as the bandits of the black wood and the red-headed robbers of Mawddwy who, in the lawless days of the Wars of the Roses, killed, burned and rustled cattle. On Christmas Eve 1554 eighty of them were rounded up and condemned to death. Among them were two brothers whose mother begged the judge, Baron Lewis Owen, to spare one of them; when he refused the mother bared her bosom and screamed, "These yellow breasts have given suck to those who shall wash their hands in your blood." It was no idle threat. The next year, as the judge rode towards Welshpool, he was ambushed on a hairpin bend at a place since called Llidiart y Barwn (Baron's gate). The outlaws blocked the road with trees and showered the judge's party with arrows, one of which hit him in the face. Owen's servants fled, the bandits moved in for the kill with spears and he was despatched by dozens of stab wounds. Dread of the bandits of Mawddwy lived on long after they had been hunted down and extirpated – the law-abiding inhabitants of the region made a custom of discouraging surprise visitors by putting a scythe blade up the chimney when they went to bed.

The death of the Yorkist Earl of Pembroke and his brother, Sir Richard Herbert, in 1469 was, according to tradition, the fulfilment of a curse. The earl had rounded up a gang of seven murderous robbers, all brothers, in Anglesey and sentenced them to hang. When the widowed mother's pleas that one son should be spared were ignored she cursed the earl with the words, "A great lord thou art, but beware when next ye hear the cry of battle lest thy neck also stretch and break." Memory of the old woman's curse came back to Sir Richard as he leaned on his pole-axe awaiting the enemy charge at Edgecot. "What! Doth thy great body apprehend anything that thou art so melancholy?" cried the earl to his brother. "I cannot but apprehend on your part lest the curse of the woman fall on you," replied Sir Richard. The Herbert forces were scattered, the earl and his brother taken prisoner and beheaded.

A thief without a bloodthirsty reputation who was too clever to get his neck in a hangman's noose was Tom Jones, better known in folklore as Twm Shon Catti (Tom Jones, Cathy's son). This 16th century son of

Dolwyddelan Castle, one of Snowdonia's ancient sentinels and birthplace of Prince Llywelyn the Great.

Tregaron (a place not quite as big as London but famed for its ham was how it was described to novelist George Borrow) became the subject of many amusing tales. In legend he was a Welsh Robin Hood, so likeable and good-natured that he rose from cut-purse to magistrate, mayor of Brecon and High Sheriff of Carmarthen, amassing a fortune and marrying an heiress on the way. Borrow, who slept in Llandovery's Castle Hotel four-poster during the travels he recorded in 'Wild Wales', tells of a shoplifting stunt in that town. Twm wanted a new porridge pot and an ironmonger obligingly produced several for inspection. Cunning Twm picked one up, complained that it had a hole in it and returned it for the disbelieving shopkeeper to study at close quarters. As the ironmonger peered into the pot, Twm jammed it down over the man's eyes, grabbed the other pots and departed with the words, "Friend, I suppose you now see that there is a hole in the pot, otherwise how else could you have got your head inside?" In another escapade he outwitted a rival highwayman. In threadbare clothes and with purses filled with seashells, Twm rode a broken-winded old nag along the lonely road where the robber operated. The highwayman duly appeared and Twm, displaying suitable fright, tossed his money-bags over the hedge. While the bandit scrambled after his haul Twm nimbly switched horses and galloped away on the robber's sleek stallion with gold coins jingling in well-filled saddlebags to his hideout cave at Ystradffin.

When Thomas Pennant recorded his journeyings he noted disappointedly his failure to find the best hunter, shooter, fisher and wrestler of the time at home in Llanberis. The person he had sought, "the last specimen of the strength and spirit of the antient British", was then 90 years old and recently wed; but being endowed with superlative skills as musician, blacksmith, boatbuilder, carpenter, shoemaker and harp-maker, Margaret of Penllyn's absence was not surprising. "She killed more foxes in one year than all the confederate hunts do in ten: rowed stoutly and was queen of the lake: fiddled excellently, and knew all our old music: did not neglect the mechanic arts, for she was a very good joiner: and, at the age of seventy, was the best wrestler in the country, and few young men dared to try a fall with her," wrote Pennant. He added that this noted Amazon who lived to be well over 100 had wed when her companion maid died, giving her hand "to the most effeminate of her admirers, as if predetermined to maintain the superiority which nature had bestowed on her."

The myths and folktales of Wales have been a rich source for writers. Shakespeare wove them into his plays knowing that many in his London audiences would recognise the references. In 'Henry the Fifth' Fluellen takes great pride in the fact that the king was born in Monmouth Castle and he avenges Pistol's insult by making the braggart eat a leek. Pistol calls Fluellen a 'base Troyan', so recalling Geoffrey of Monmouth's claim that the Britons were descended from a band of refugee Trojans led by Brutus, and when Fluellen presses the vegetable on him Pistol cries, "Not for Cadwallader and all his goats." Cadwaladr was a young goatherd whose best nanny ran off and he gave chase along ravines and up slopes with the goat leading him ever higher into the mountains. Exasperated by the elusive animal he picked up a rock and threw it at the runaway. His aim was good and the hit sent the goat tumbling over a cliff. Cadwaladr climbed down to the sorely wounded creature which, in tearful remorse, he cradled in his arms. Day faded into night and when the full moon rose above the peaks the goat was transformed into an enticing maiden.

Henry of Monmouth learned many martial lessons as a teenager in Wales while fighting a man whose aim was to free the country of English rule. Prince Hal's adversary in the early years of the 15th century was Owain Glyndwr, a man whose name and deeds rapidly acquired fabulous repute. While Hal's father, Henry IV, considered by many to be a usurper, strove to establish his rule, Glyndwr expelled the English from much of Wales, seized several of their castles, Conwy, Harlech, Aberystwyth and Cilgerran among them, and defeated the armies sent against him –

> *Three times hath Henry Bolingbroke made head*
> *Against my power: thrice from the banks of the Wye*
> *And sandy-bottom'd Severn have I sent him*
> *Bootless home and weather-beaten back.*

Glyndwr's own strongholds were at Sycharth near Llansilin and 'Glyndwr's Mount' near Corwen. According to tradition, Owain left his mark on Corwen Church, one of several Welsh churches which legend says had problems until the builders obeyed supernatural signs and built on the correct Heaven-designated site. The lintel above one of Corwen Church's doorways is marked by a dagger-shaped incision said to have been made when the hero threw his sword from a nearby hill.

A land dispute with Lord Grey of Ruthin sparked Owain's rebellion in 1400 and soon his struggle became a national crusade for independence. Ruthin was sacked and Grey captured when he unwisely ventured beyond the safety of his castle walls; he was locked up in the old Welsh castle of Dolbadarn until a ransom purchased his release. Owain gained another high-born captive in 1402 when, at Pilleth just west of Offa's Dyke, his forces gained a famous victory over an army led by Sir Edmund Mortimer – Shakespeare's 'revolted Mortimer' – who changed his allegiance, married his captor's daughter and then plotted with Owain and his brother-in-law Hotspur (Henry Percy) to topple Henry IV off his throne and carve up the kingdom among themselves. In a Shakespearean scene of the allies meeting at Bangor to discuss their plans, Hotspur mocks the Welsh prince . . .

> *sometimes he angers me*
> *With telling me of the moldwarp and the ant,*
> *Of the dreamer Merlin and his prophecies,*
> *And of a dragon, and a finless fish,*
> *A clip-wing'd griffin, and a moulten raven,*
> *A couching lion, and a rampaging cat,*

And such a deal of skimble-skamble stuff
As puts me from my faith. I'll tell thee what;
He held me last night at least nine hours
In reckoning up the several devils' names
That were his lackeys.

Among these allusions to Welsh mythology the ant refers to the enduring Mabinogion tale of Culhwch and the 40 tasks he had to perform before he could marry Olwen. One labour was to retrieve nine bushels of flax seed which had been sown in a field. Fortunately one of King Arthur's knights saved a colony of ants from a fire and the grateful insects did the work, the last seed being brought in at sundown by one of their lame brethren. Owain's enemies thought he had wizard powers and Shakespeare's Glendower repeats how dreadful omens had accompanied his birth –

Give me leave
To tell you once again that at my birth
The front of heaven was full of fiery shapes,
The goats ran from the mountains, and the herds
Were strangely clamorous to the frighted fields.
These signs have mark'd me extraordinary;

Indeed Glyndwr was 'not in the roll of common men' and in 1403 he and Hotspur almost changed the course of English and Welsh history. The plan was that they should combine against Prince Hal at Shrewsbury but King Henry hastened with his army to join his son and together they confronted Hotspur's troops before the Welsh arrived. Traditionally it is said that Glyndwr could not cross the rain-swollen Severn and had to watch the battle in which he was helpless to intervene while perched in an oak tree on the other side of the river. Hotspur was killed and Henry IV marked his success by building Battlesfield Church as a chantry where prayers could be offered for the souls of those slain in the fight.

Owain was proclaimed Prince of Wales, he summoned Welsh Parliaments, and made a treaty with the King of France who sent troops to aid attacks on Henry's castles, but the tide of events ran in favour of the English. Glyndwr's power waned and Mortimer, whose tomb effigy is in Montgomery Church, died of starvation in besieged Harlech Castle. Owain vanished from history into legend; Henry V offered pardon but there was no reply. Where and when Owain died nobody knows though Monnington-on-Wye claims to be the place of his death in 1415 while another tradition links him with Grosmont where the figure of a knight in the church was said to be his effigy. Across the river from Grosmont's church and castle (one of the strongholds besieged by Owain) is Kentchurch where the Scudamore family ruled and with whom Owain is said to have taken refuge – one of his daughters had married into the family. Legend says that he lived out a long life in the alias of a parish priest known as John of Kentchurch.

Folklore has other tales to tell of Owain. Below Moel Hebog is a cave, Ogof Owain Glyndwr, where he and his warriors took refuge; and legend asserts that he rests, like King Arthur, in a secret cavern awaiting the summons to return. Dafydd ap Llywelyn of Brecon (Davy Gam in Henry V), Glyndwr's kinsman and the supposed model for Shakespeare's Fluellen, is said to have plotted to kill Owain at the Machynlleth Parliament in 1404. On the eve of Agincourt Henry V asked Gam the numbers of the French army and the fearless red-haired warrior said that there were enough to be slain, enough to be taken prisoner and enough to run away. He was listed among Henry's 'English dead' of the victory of 1415, the year that Owain is said to have expired in hiding, and tradition claims that the king knighted the dying Davy Gam on the battlefield. Another of Owain's would-be assassins and kinsmen was Hywel Sele who tried to put an arrow in his guest's back while they hunted in the hills near Cymmer Abbey. Alternatively it is said that Owain killed cousin Hywel, lord of Nannau, because he would not join the fight against the English. Whatever the motive, the story is that Glyndwr concealed the body in a hollow, lightning-scorched oak and that years later, as he lay dying, he ordered a loyal follower to ride to Nannau to reveal Hywel's fate to the widow who harboured hopes that her husband was alive. Hywel's skeleton, rusty sword in hand, was found in the 'hollow oak of demonrie' and then in 1813, to confound the belief that lightning never strikes twice, the blasted tree was blasted again and fell. But the toppling of the old oak did not quieten Hywel's restless spirit because on anniversary nights of his death a blood-chilling, mournful moan can be heard emanating from the lonely hills.

Power struggles and feuds between the Welsh princes, often between brothers, fathers and sons, sapped the power to resist the expansive ambitions of English Marcher barons and kings. Gwynedd was the last principality to succumb when Edward I, enraged by a surprise night attack on Hawarden Castle, mobilised large land and sea forces for a campaign of conquest in 1282. Five years earlier Llywelyn of Gwynedd had lost his lands beyond Snowdonia and Anglesey but when his hot-blooded brother, Dafydd, the man who had kidnapped Llywelyn's bride-to-be, stormed Hawarden he joined the fight against the English overlords. Legend has added its own dimensions to the death of Llywelyn the Last in a skirmish at Cilmeri. The garrison of nearby Builth Castle refused to help the prince who was surprised and killed by a Welsh soldier in English pay. Folklore has it that a blacksmith had reversed the shoes of Llywelyn's horse so that a false trail would be left in the snow but he betrayed the secret to the Mortimers. Another tale is that broom was unseasonably in flower at the time and the wounded prince was battered to death with a broomstick and since then no broom would grow on the spot.

The last of the House of Gwynedd's male line died almost a century later, killed like many of his predecessors by an assassin's hand. He was Owain ap Thomas (Froissart's Yvan of Wales, 'a man gretly behated in England') whose attempts to return with a fleet supplied by the French king were thwarted by the weather. His killer, James Lambe 'out of the

*The circular keep of Dolbadarn Castle in the shadow of
Snowdon was once the jail of noble prisoners.*

Marches of Wales', was 'but a small gentylman, and that well shewed after, for a very gentylman wyll never set his mynde on so evyll an entent.' Lambe found Owain busy besieging a castle at Mortain and won his trust 'for he made him beleve howe all the countre of Wales wolde gladlye have hym to be their lorde'. One morning Owain sent Lambe to fetch his comb 'and as he was comyng, I trowe the devyll entered into hym, for besyde the combe he brought with hym a lytell javelyne of Spayne, with a large heed of stele, and with the same strake this Yvan as he sate, clene through out the body so that he fell down starke deed'. Many refused to believe he was dead and it was said he (or an earlier warrior Owain who fought the Saxons) rests in a Black Mountains cavern near Llandeilo.

Omens, signs and portents had a powerful hold on the minds of medieval men and one, recorded by the chronicler Jean Froissart, was witnessed by 30,000 men at a confrontation whose bitter fruit was the Wars of the Roses – a dynastic struggle which ended when, as Merlin had predicted, a Welshman gained the English throne. In 1399 Henry Bolingbroke, Duke of Lancaster, was in arms against Richard II who sought safety in Conwy Castle. Assured by the oaths of an earl and an archbishop that he would keep his crown, Richard rode forth into an ambush at Penmaenrhos and was hurried off to Flint where Bolingbroke was waiting and a dog signalled his downfall. The dog was Math, Richard's favourite hunting greyhound which, when unleashed, would run to him and not leave his side. But when Richard came face to face with the usurper the dog ran past him to the uncrowned Henry IV, stood up on its back legs with front paws on his shoulders 'paying him every court'. The startled face-licked Henry asked the meaning of the dog's fondness and Richard resignedly told him, "This greyhound fondles and pays his court to you this day as King of England, which you will surely be, and I shall be deposed." So Merlin's warning that a king who had ruled for 20 years would fall in a triangular place was proved correct – the walls built to protect Conwy gave the medieval town a triangular boundary.

The Merlin prophecy which Welshmen most wanted fulfilled was victory for the red dragon of Wales over the white dragon of England and in 1485 the crowning of Henry VII, the first of the Tudor kings, was interpreted by many as the achievement of that prediction. In two generations, while the English nobility murdered, executed and killed each other in the Wars of the Roses, the family of a modest Anglesey landowner climbed over them all to take the throne. Owain Tewdwr of Penmynydd secretly wedded Henry V's widow, Catherine of Valois, but when word of the Welsh squire's upstart marriage to the still young queen-mother got abroad he was cast into jail. Eventually the scandal died and Henry VI showed Owain's sons and his half-brothers, Edmund and Jasper, royal favour by giving them the earldoms of Richmond and Pembroke. Edmund Tudor married young Margaret Beaufort, a member of the only surviving branch of the Lancastrian line, and at 15 years old and with her husband dead she gave birth in Pembroke Castle to the future Henry VII.

His journey to the crown was perilous. In 1461 grandfather Owain was beheaded at Hereford after his son Jasper's defeat at Mortimer's Cross, and as a boy Henry was caught up in the siege of Harlech. In 1471, after Tewkesbury fight, he became the Lancastrian claimant to the throne and he and his mentor, uncle Jasper, were forced to flee. Henry eluded Richard III's men at Mostyn Hall by jumping out of a window; when the captain of the king's men asked why there was an extra place at the dinner table he was told it was an hospitable custom to be prepared for surprise guests, an offer of which the suspicious soldier availed himself. In Brittany Henry narrowly escaped a plot to have him shipped back to face Richard's tender mercies, then, against an August sunset in 1485, he and Jasper sailed into Mill Bay to begin the march to Bosworth field. A few miles up the road Rhys ap Thomas semantically honoured his pledge to Richard that Henry would pass only over his body – he stood under Mullock Bridge while the invader rode over his head. Rhys, whose noted duellist father was treacherously killed as he was getting his breath back after a fight of honour, joined Henry's cause and it is said that he was the man who slew King Richard as, no doubt, the doomed monarch was offering his kingdom for a horse. It is said that on the way to Bosworth Henry stayed a night at Aber-Ffrydlan as guest of a man noted for his powers of prediction. Henry asked his host how he saw the future and the seer assured him that everything looked rosy. As Henry rode away to his destiny the prophet explained to his wife that if their visitor won they might be well rewarded, but if he lost a dead claimant to the throne would not seek redress.

A few months later Henry VII wed Elizabeth of York and the kingdom would have had a genuine King Arthur had their eldest son not died at 15. Instead England and Wales got greedy, despotic, luxury-loving Henry VIII. He cared nothing for his Welsh ancestry and his 1536 Act of Union carried the words 'from henceforth no person or persons that use the Welsh speech or language shall have or enjoy any manner of office or fees within this realm of England, Wales or other the king's dominion, upon pain of forfeiting the same offices or fees unless he or they use and exercise the English speech or language.' Henry's tyranny ensured that one more prophecy came true. Llandderfel Church once had an effigy of St Derfel mounted on a horse, dating from the time when pilgrims visited the shrine of the saint who had taken to holy contemplation after fighting at King Arthur's side of Camlan. Such 'idolatrous images' were ordered to be burned at the Reformation and despite a bribe offered by the people of Llandderfel who wanted to keep their wooden saint, the object was carted off to London. There the prophecy that it would 'set a forest afire' came true because it was part of the bonfire on which Catherine of Aragon's confessor, Friar John Forest, was burned to death in 1538.

Harold's Stones at Trellech — huge markers of a king's forgotten battle or pebbles thrown by a passing giant?

Fairy lore, fairy gold, enchantment and the dread of iron's touch

"The wretched Welsh repeat their idle legends from first to second childhood, bring forward a thousand attestations to the existence of witches and fairies . . . " so wrote poet and novelist, William Savage Landor, in the early years of the 19th century. The Englishman's cynicism was fuelled, no doubt, by his money problems, quarrels with neighbours and tenants, and the failure of his grandiose scheme to restore the ruins of Llanthony Priory. An earlier writer, Welshman Edmund Jones, had little doubt that fairies existed and he recorded the observations of people who had seen and heard them. Jones, who died in 1793, said that sightings of fairy folk had been commoner in former times and an "abundance of people saw them and heard their music, which everyone said was low and pleasant, but none could ever learn the tune."

The fairies were a mysterious race. They were guardians of secrets and knowledge denied to humans and they loved to enjoy themselves in song and dance. Sometimes they assisted their mortal neighbours, often they indulged in pranks and mischievous behaviour, and on occasion they would reward a kindly deed but punish a breach of trust. The women-folk of the usually child-size race were seen less often than the men who loved to gallop on horses the size of hares. The best places to see them were near old standing stones, megaliths, castles and hillforts where the entrances to their subterranean domains were conealed. At the sound of a magic word a heavy stone would slide to reveal a tunnel to fairyland.

The fairies' moonlit revels were betrayed by rings in the grass – the marks of their dancing feet. To step into a fairy ring and join them in their dance was an act fraught with peril according to folklore tales of those who ignored the warnings of their elders and succumbed to the bewitching music. "When they appeared like dancing companies, they were desirous to entice persons into their companies, and some were drawn among them and remained among them some time; usually a whole year, as did a man whom I knew well, and was a neighbour, who came back at the year's end, and looked very bad. But either they were not able to give much account of themselves or they durst not give it, and only said they had been dancing and that the time was short," wrote Jones.

Those who did join a fairy dance and managed to return would find to their amazement that their neighbours swore they had been absent for a year and a day although, to the participant, it seemed but a few hours. Others were victims of a crueller fate when they returned to the human world. They could discover no living relative or acquaintance; their homes were occupied by strangers; where there had been saplings there were full-grown trees; all had changed except the mountains and rivers. And when they approached a stranger for an explanation a touch would transform the dancer into ancient dust soon blown away by the wind. A farmer of Gwynedd lost his comely daughter when she was enticed to link hands with a circle of fairy dancers. When a month had passed and a full moon shone again, the father and the dozen strongest men of the parish waited till they heard the music, then, tying one end of a rope around himself, the farmer darted into the ring, grabbed his daughter tightly about the waist and the brawny twelve heaved them clear.

Two shepherds of Llanbadarn Fynydd, friends since boyhood, were walking home one evening when, from one of a trio of tumuli, they heard the sounds of music and laughter. They still had three miles to go and already the western sky was dimming with the setting sun. One, who had a new young wife at home, urged his companion to ignore the fairy revels but unmarried Dic lingered and listened. "Come on, Dic, no good will come of it," the newly-wed called, but Dic, undeterred, turned towards the source of the music and shouted that he would soon catch up. Next day there was no sign of Dic and as the days passed a whispered rumour began to circulate that Dic was dead, murdered, and the main suspect was his life-long friend. The weeks became months and Dic still failed to appear, and murmured misgivings intensified to such degree that the squire arrested the innocent friend and cast him into jail with iron fetters on arms and legs. The prisoner's wife, fearing that she might become a young widow not a twelve-month from her wedding day, climbed the hill to Castell-y-blaidd where an old, white-bearded man renowned for his knowledge of fairy ways lived alone. He heard her tale and instructed her to return with magistrate, squire, parish constable and seven strong men to the place where Dic had last been seen. But magistrate and squire were men whose Oxford learning made them contemptuous of talk of fairies. Each day she tearfully pleaded her cause until, at last, their hearts softened by one so fair, they agreed to go with her to the moors and listen for fairy music.

It was a year and a day exactly since Dic had vanished when the party climbed towards the ridge with those three grassy mounds. The evening breeze bore the sound of music towards them and, as they cleared the final rise, they saw Dic cavorting hand-in-hand in a circle of little people. The seven strong men formed a human chain, grabbed Dic as he came whirling past and sent him tumbling down the bank. He laughed in disbelief when magistrate and squire, converted to the truth of fairies, harangued him about his foolishness which had almost sent an innocent friend to the gallows. "That can't be true, it is not 10 minutes since we parted," he protested. Pointing to a western sky still streaked with day he exclaimed, "See, the sky is still yet light!" Dic was finally convinced when his friend came home with shackle marks on wrists and ankles, and never again, when he heard enticing music in the hills, did he bend his path to investigate. And to mark his 'ten-minute dance' which lasted a year and a day one of those three old earth mounds still bears his name.

Many ancient standing stones and barrows which are the claimed haunts of fairies are themselves the subjects of folktales. A barrow near the scene of St Germanus' 'Alleluia victory' is said to be the haunt of a giant with golden armour who jealously guards the treasure of a king killed in battle; a standing stone on Anglesey is an everlasting warning against greed because it is explained as being the petrified form of a thief who stole a sacred object from a nearby church; the stones of the Druids' Circle above Penmaenmawr are associated with ancient goddesses while others say they are women turned to stone for ignoring a holy man's warning against gossiping on Sundays. The largest of the stones avenges blasphemy and bad language by giving offenders a stunning clout.

Hugh of Montgomery, Earl of Shrewsbury, learned of the power of stones when he invaded Anglesey in 1098. He was told of a stone shaped like a thigh bone which always returned to its original site and so, to test the truth of the tale, he had it chained to a larger stone and thrown into the sea. But iron chains could not defeat the supernatural and, sure enough, next morning the stone was back in the spot where it had always been. Hugh gave orders that no-one should meddle with it again. The site of the magic stone was a popular place for lovers' trysts – not only did the stone sweat during their love-making but its convenient contraceptive properties ensured that no baby would result from the sexual union. Hugh and his fellow Norman invaders were expelled from Anglesey in an ironic twist of history. In 1098 Magnus Bareleg, King of Norway, sailed his fleet into the Menai Strait (the Anglo-Saxon Chronicle calls them pirates) and Hugh, iron-clad from head to foot and riding his charger along the shore, was killed, like King Harold at Hastings, by an arrow in the eye (Hugh in the right eye and Harold in the left according to Gerald of Wales). The missile which found the chink in Hugh's armour was fired by Magnus, son of Harold Hardrada who had been killed in battle against King Harold at Stamford Bridge, and one of his fellow 'pirates' was that King Harold's son. Earl Hugh's death was seen as divine judgement because a few days earlier he had sacrilegiously kennelled his hounds, which went raving mad overnight, in Llandyfrydog church.

King Harold is remembered by a trio of standing stones at Trellech. One tradition says they are a memorial to a battle he won there and that those killed in the fight were buried at Tump Terrett which is really the motte of a Norman castle. A 17th century sundial in the church is carved with pictures of Harold's Stones, the mound and a local holy spring which had a reputation for curing ills and was known as the Virtuous Well. Another claim is that the stones, more than eight feet high, were 'pebbles' thrown by a passing giant. Harold is said to have had a 'castle' at Walton where the Four Stones, traditionally the grave-markers of four battle-slain kings, answer the call of Old Radnor's church bells by marching off to a nearby pond for a drink.

A farmer of Ardudwy learned to his cost that moving a standing stone could have spectacular results. The stone stood in the middle of a field on a hillside behind his home and he determined to remove the obstacle to his ploughing. The fairies, who could overhear the words of human discussion borne on the wind, warned against the project but the stubborn farmer took no heed. On the chosen spring morning the farmer entered the field with his oxen, but before he could hitch the team to the stone it toppled over and went rolling down the slope. At first the farmer watched in horror as the boulder gathered momentum and headed towards his house, then, to his relief, it bounded past the door and splashed into the river. But his elation at having accomplished his task without effort was soon washed away – the mighty stone diverted the flow to a new course and the water rushed through the house, in at the front door and out at the back, carrying pots and pans and furniture with it. And from the hills above he could hear the scornful laughter of fairy voices. Other tales tell of standing stones which have resisted the muscle power of men and oxen only to move at the touch of a pure-hearted maiden who discovered a crock of gold to transform the life and fortune of her poor family. Two prehistoric burial chambers near Barry gave rise to a crop of tales. As well as being the haunt of fairies, the stones of Tinkinswood are controlled by the spirits of long dead druids – they chastise drunken sinners and while those who dare to sleep on its 40-ton capstone on mid-summer eve may be made poets the capricious spirits may, with equal facility, turn the dreamers mad. At neaby St Lythan is another old tomb with massive capstone held aloft by three stones. Here the spirits of pagan priests make the capstone twirl on the eve of the summer solstice. Many stones from prehistoric ages were credited with the power of locomotion (going to drink or bathe in nearby rivers is a common tradition) and there are other tales to explain their situation. Some are said to be travellers turned to stone by demonic spirits which haunt the roads at night, some are fairy fiddlers and dancers who come to life by moonlight, and some mark the graves of poets, warriors, and saints. Others are fossilised bodies of women (in folklore it is always women) whose scandalmongering sent an innocent to jail or gibbet, and some will grant a maiden's soft-spoken wish on Lady's Day eve – women of maturer years had to make their requests on Hallowe'en. The village of Maentwrog takes its name from 'Twrog's stone' which stands in the churchyard where its has rested since the saint hurled it from a mountain top to smash a pagan shrine (his 'finger-prints' are still on it).

The sea-girt peninsula of Gower has numerous relics of prehistory. There are ancient burial chambers, hill and cliff forts, and caves which have yielded the bones of mammoths, elephants and bison. In 1823 the skeleton of the 'Red Lady of Paviland' was discovered in a cave and it was said she was an unfortunate woman trapped by a storm while hunting for buried treasure. In fact 'she' was a man who died more than 18,000 years ago. The caves of coasts and mountains have tales of hidden treasure and sleeping warriors as well as a common folkloric theme of vanished musicians. The caves of Great Ormes Head, Craig Ddu near Criccieth and Bullslaughter Bay near Bosherton are among those into which explorers have ventured, sometimes enticed by fairies, never to be

Tinkinswood burial chamber – the haunt of fairies and guardian of strange powers over daring sleepers.

*Pentre Ifan cromlech south of Cardigan is one of many
Welsh prehistoric sites where fairies have been seen.*

seen again by their fellow men, although their music can still be heard issuing from a secret subterranean haunt where they fiddle and pipe their tunes through timeless eternity. The only survivor of these escapades was said to be a dog which never again ventured near the cave.

Gerald of Wales recorded the tale of a priest who had passed many days in the mysterious world of fairies. As a boy, Elidyr ran away from school and met two men of small stature who took him to a land of magical delights. They entered a secret passage near a river bank and emerged into a realm of bountiful rivers and lush meadows but it was a land where even at noon it was dim and shadowy, and at night there were no moon or stars overhead. The stranger was conducted to the royal court of the fairies where he marvelled at the riches of gold and soon befriended the king's young son. Elidyr became a trusted companion, and he learned the customs of his hosts who made plain their abhorrence of human deceit and faithlessness caused by greed and ambition. Occasionally Elidyr, who knew the secret of the hidden passage, would return to the world above ground to see his mother and when she heard his tales she persuaded him to steal some fairy gold. One day he grabbed the fairy prince's golden ball and headed for home but just as he reached the front door he tripped, dropped it and pursuing fairies retrieved the prize. Never again did Elidyr find the entrance to the tunnel that led to fairyland.

Another man learned to regret the day he found fairy gold. By chance he had pronounced the password which caused a stone to move to reveal a tunnel. Adventurously he took his chance, followed a candle-lit path and emerged into a cavern filled with treasure. But he neglected to replace the entrance stone and a draught of wind extinguished the candles to alert the fairies to the intruder's presence. The unfortunate man was never seen again by humankind so it was assumed he was taken prisoner.

Treasure-hunter John had a narrow escape when he agreed to help a magician seek gold hidden beneath Mynydd y Drum. At midnight by the light of a full moon, the wizard marked two circles on the ground and warned John that on no account must he step outside his ring while the spells were cast. The magic was frighteningly potent and the conjured apparitions made John recoil and cross the line. Instantly the Devil appeared in a cloud of sulphurous smoke and was about to convey the unlucky wobbler to Hell when the wizard intervened. He produced the stub of a candle from his pocket, lit it and tricked the lord high demon into agreeing that John could remain in this world for as long as the stub lasted. With a smile the wizard pinched out the flame and John ran home not caring that his treasure-hunting days were over.

One evening an elderly shepherd was returning to his home beneath the slopes of Cefn Cenarth near St Harmon (an area of many Bronze Age burial mounds) and as he approached two old standing stones near the river which marked his way home – one is now fallen over – he saw three small figures dressed in green. The trio told him that they had travelled far that day and were tired, hungry and thirsty. The kindly old man, thinking they were children, produced some bread and cheese which was gratefully accepted, and then he brought them water from the river in his cap. That night the shepherd's sleep was broken by a soft but persistent knocking on the door. When he opened it he saw in the moonlight the three fair faces of the 'children' he had encountered earlier but this time he recognised them as fairies, and there were more of them peering over walls and from behind trees. One stepped forward and told the old man that they had come to repay his kindness; they would grant him any wish he cared to make. Though poor the man was content with his life so, after a long pause, he whispered his wish into the fairy's ear. He watched until the file of little people had disappeared into the darkness of the night then, as he turned, he saw that his wish had already come true – in the doorway was a golden harp glinting in the moonlight.

Next day his wife berated him for a fool. Why had he not asked for purses filled with gold, piles of precious gems, or fine clothes of silk and fur? "Woman, we have no need of such things. I am a shepherd and I live by the seasons. Now we shall have music and no king can tax our song, our laughter or our dance. This night you, I and our neighbours shall sing, laugh and dance as never before," he replied. Through the dark hours the cottage rang with music and laughter, for when he ran his rough fingers over the strings the golden harp made music sweeter than anyone had ever heard, and such was the merriment within the house that no-one noticed the little faces which occasionally appeared at the windows. None could resist the music – men and women, old and young, fat and thin, the sexton's sour-faced wife and the blacksmith's unsmiling spinster daughter, all whirled and twirled till dawn when the shepherd laid the harp aside. The dancers groaned with exhaustion and hobbled away home, some with blistered feet, many had bruised soles, others nursed sprains and strains. For three days all who lived between Llanidloes and Rhayader, Llangurig and Llanbister slept, no-one went to work, except the shepherd.

The sexton dug no graves, the baker baked no bread and the blacksmith shod no horses. When aches and pains faded, the men grumbled and the women gossiped; the old shepherd had bewitched them with his harp they said. When the fairies heard how people spoke of their friend they decided to act – the golden harp vanished and in its place the shepherd found a single golden guinea. He took his wife to Llanidloes market where he brought her new stockings, shawl and bonnet, and when they got home, there on the kitchen table, was another guinea. Once a week, each and every week, they journeyed to market but never did they spend more than one golden guinea, except for the time when the old shepherd took his savings and made a special purchase. His fingers could not make his new harp sing like the golden one, but never again did his neighbours dance till dawn or suffer swollen feet.

Fairy magic had no defence against iron, a metal dreaded by the little people. An infallible method of preventing child-stealing pranks by mischievous fairies who had the cuckoo habit of swapping human babes for their own, was to place an iron object in an infant's cradle. Mothers whose babes would not grow soon suspected that they were rearing fairy changelings. A farmer and his wife of Trefeglwys had twin sons who, despite diligent attention and the constant satisfaction of voracious appetites, failed to magnify and mature. The worried wife consulted an old man who was known to be wise in such matters and on his advice prepared just enough food to fill an empty egg-shell which, she declared, would feed the men in the fields when they returned from their harvest labours. "Acorns before oaks I know, an egg before a hen, but never would one hen's egg-shell of stew satisfy harvest men," cried the gluttonous pair of hobgoblins. The wife snatched the two greedy-guts from their warm bed, dumped them in a wheelbarrow and charged up the hill towards Llyn Ebyr. As she held the counterfeit children by the scruffs of their necks ready to throw them into the dark water, a wailing cry rose from the ramparts of Pen y Castell on the ridge above. There stood a group of fairies ready to exchange two lively toddlers for their own indolent brats. Another couple tempted fate by delaying the christening of their new-born son – fairies would never abduct a baptised babe – and had the infant stolen while they slept. But they soon forced its return. The husband sprinkled salt on a spade's iron blade, drew the sign of a cross and held it over the flames of the kitchen fire. Within minutes there was a tap on the window and the child was found in its swaddling clothes on the doorstep. At noon the vicar held the child at the church font and made the sign of a cross on the babe's wet forehead.

Mixed marriages between humans and fairies were doomed to end in heartbreak. Several tales tell of men who wooed and won a fairy bride, the couples living happily together until the fateful day when the wife was touched by iron. Such was the destiny of a handsome young man who lived near Llyn Cwellyn in Snowdonia. One night he glimpsed a vision of loveliness in the moonlight and night after night he returned to the same spot hoping to see the beautiful maiden again. His persistence and patience were eventually rewarded when the fairy appeared but this time he grasped her around the waist and carried her off to his home. Despite all his entreaties of love, however, she refused to become his wife saying that she would live as his maid-servant if he would address her by name. Day after day he tried every feminine name he knew and each time she would shake her head. Then, one day, he saw a group of seven fairies crouched in a circle in animated discussion. Stealthily he drew near and eavesdropped on their discussion – they spoke of a fairy maiden who was living in the human world. Home he rushed and called out the name 'Penelope'. "You have discovered my secret, I shall be true to my word," she replied and using the powers known only to her race the young man's cows remained healthy when those of his neighbours sickened with murrain; soon he had an excess of the finest butter and cheese to sell at market. Each day through the ensuing four seasons he asked Penelope to marry him and each day she refused. A year and day passed from the time he had first spoken her true name until the day she consented to become his bride, but her acceptance of his proposal was on condition that never would she be struck by iron. He readily agreed and joyous were the celebrations which followed the wedding and so great was their happiness that all said it was a true love-match.

As man and wife they prospered beyond his wildest imaginings and soon they and their growing family occupied one of the finest houses in Arfon. Then dawned the fateful day. He planned to ride to Caernarfon fair and, with the sun already high, he was impatient to begin his journey. He went to saddle his horse but the beast was spirited and frisky, so he called to Penelope to help him calm the animal. As she came running to his assistance, the horse slipped from its halter and galloped away; in frustration he hurled the bridle after it and the harness with an iron bit struck his fairy wife. Instantly she vanished from his sight. House and farm decayed; his prosperity withered away; the man who had been the happiest and most fortunate of husbands wandered the hills, his heart filled with remorse, crying out the name Penelope. The only reply that came to his ears was the soft whisper of the wind, the gentle tumbling of clear mountain streams and the occasional echoed name of the wife he had lost forever.

A man of renown who married a stunningly beautiful fairy bride was Eadric the Wild. He was an English nobleman with estates along the Powys Marches near Wigmore who, with the aid of Welsh princes, attacked the castles of the Norman conquerors at Shrewsbury and Hereford and plundered the towns. Walter Map, a Herefordshire-born clerical chronicler of 12th century court gossip, recorded the story of Eadric's impulsive and forcible abduction of the highly desirable creature. One night he was returning to his manor at Lydbury North after a hunting trip when he got lost in the woods. He came upon a large house in which he saw some seductively clad maidens enjoying a dance. Among this array of feminine beauty – they were all taller and more attractive than human women – Eadric was 'wounded to the heart' by one whose face and figure were finer than those of any king's mistress. The warrior-lord burst in, grabbed her and carried her away. For three days and three nights she surrendered silently to his passion. On the fourth day she broke her silence, saying he would enjoy good health and prosperity as long as he uttered no reproachful remark about her sisters. Eadric gave his promise, avowed his undying love and amid great rejoicing they became man and wife.

Word of the unmatched beauty of Eadric's bride spread through the land and William the Conqueror summoned them to his court in London. All who saw her said she was comely beyond compare which was proof of her fairy origin. The years went by until, as in all tales of fairy brides, one moment of thoughtless impatience resulted in years of sorrow. Eadric came home late one night from a hunt (the heroes of legend spent a lot of time indulging their passion for chasing wild game)

The peaks of Yr Eifl in Lleyn, one is topped by the ancient hillfort of Tre'r Ceiri (the town of giants).

and he failed to find his wife meekly awaiting his return. Angered by her delay in answering his summons, Eadric turned on her and sneered, "Doubtless, madam, you had business with your sisters!" The words had hardly left his lips before this wife of incomparable beauty vanished for ever from the sight of humankind. All Eadric's tears of remorse, cries of repentance and appeals for pardon were in vain and he died, said the chronicler, of a broken heart. Wild Eadric and his fairy wife left a son who, when he grew old, was stricken with palsy which was cured when he prayed at the shrine of St Ethelbert in Hereford Cathedral.

Another chronicler claims that Eadric was besieged in Wigmore Castle by Normans and delivered in chains to William the Conqueror who caused the Saxon rebel to end his days in a dungeon. Legend tells that Eadric, whose sword is hidden in the depths of a pool near Shrewsbury, lives on in old lead-mines near The Long Mynd where his knocks and tappings led miners to the richest finds. Sometimes he appears above ground in the guise of a fiery-eyed hound and others have spied him mounted on a white stallion, blowing his hunting horn as a warning of the approach of war. His golden-haired wife rides beside him at the head of his war-band and all of them are dressed in cloaks of fairy green.

In legend, as in life, to see is not necessarily to believe, particularly when magic is involved. Many wayfarers have been duped by fairy mirages. They have seen the welcoming lights of an inn where never one had been before, enjoyed the warmth of fire, the taste of fine victuals and beer, slept soundly in a soft bed of down, and then woken cold and dewy-damp at dawn under a hedge or in the company of hogs. A more sober-sided tale is that of a midwife of Nant Peris (several similar versions have other locations) who accidentally attained the dubious gift of fairy sight. Her tale began one evening as she sat spinning by her fireside. An insistent knocking at her door revealed a man, nay, a nobleman if he be judged by his fine clothes and the heavy purse on his belt. He explained that his wife had urgent need of the old lady's midwifery skills and together they rode off on his horse. The grandam closed her eyes as they galloped through the darkness until the stranger reined-in at the entrance to a grand palace. Never had she seen such grandeur – its wall were mightier and its towers taller than those of the king's castles at Conwy and Caernarfon. He led her to a luxuriously appointed bedchamber where a beautiful young woman lay close to childbirth. Rich tapestries hung from the walls and the light of a hundred candles was reflected by furniture of gold and silver. The midwife calmed the couple's anxieties and a healthy child was delivered into the world, whereupon the husband produced a phial of ointment with which the old woman was instructed to bathe the babe's eyes. But, warned the husband, on no account was the potion to touch her own eyes. As she carried the child towards a table with basin and pitcher of beaten gold, the old woman felt an itch and inadvertently brushed one of her eyes with the liquid.

Immediately a new and distressing scene was revealed. Where there had been carpets she saw a stamped-earth floor, instead of fine draperies there were damp cave walls, and the wife lay not upon a golden bed but on foul and matted straw. The midwife completed her chores and great was her relief when she regained her humble cottage as dawn streaked the eastern sky. Several days later the old lady packed up her new-spun yarns and took them to Caernarfon market. As she dawdled among the stalls she noticed the stranger among the crowd and allowed her matronly instincts to get the better of her silence. "How fare your wife and child?" she asked. The man replied that both were in perfect health, and then, looking down into the old woman's face, he asked, "Which eye is it that sees me?" Unsuspectingly the midwife indicated her right eye and in an instant the man took a stick and jabbed the fairy-sighted eye into blindness.

Usually, however, encounters with fairy-folk did not end with such acts of malicous disfigurement, although another old maid had embarrassing cause to regret that she ever asked the fairies to grant her a wish. Like tiresome neighbours, members of the local fairy colony were constantly borrowing her pots and pans and baking bowls, so she asked them to grant her a wish as recompense. The old women, who had just bought some new cloth which was a little too short and of the wrong hue for her needs, asked that whatever she touched next should be made green and half-a-yard longer. As she reached out for the cloth a fly buzzed in front of her face, she instinctively swiped at it and brushed her nose.

The pastoral economy of old Wales is echoed in fable by many references to cows and goats. A remarkably bounteous beast was 'the freckled cow' of Mynydd Hiraethog. It would contentedly fill to over-flowing the jug or pail of anyone in need, but the neighbourhood forfeited this indiscriminate largesse when a malevolent old hag put a sieve under its udder, muttered "Fill that!" and milked the perplexed creature dry. This unreasonable demand on its remarkable though finite productive capacity caused the animal to vanish. A cow of similarly generous character was the spotless white one which wandered the world bestowing its unique product to all and sundry. Those who drank its milk were cured of any ailment, the stupid were made wise and the criminal became good. But when it grazed in the Vale of Tywi the locals were not satisfied with such blessings and planned a barbecue. At the sight of the butcher's knife the indignant animal emulated its freckled sister and disappeared.

A man who certainly enjoyed good fortune through the efforts of a four-legged beast was Richard Lloyd Price whose tomb is in Llanfor churchyard. Businessman, writer and renowned sportsman, his inscription pays tribute to the swiftness of the racehorse which earned him a few guineas –

> As to my latter end I go
> To win my Jubilee,
> I bless the good horse Bendigo,
> Who built this tomb for me.

Llyn Tegid (Bala Lake) – legend says its waters flowed from an uncovered well to swamp an ancient town.

Drowned lands, shipwrecks, pirates and the legends of the lakes

Seithenyn was both a drunkard and a fool. Worse, he was the man entrusted with the task upon which depended the lives and prosperity of hundreds of men, women and children. Seithenyn had charge of the sea defences which guarded Cantref y Gwaelod (the lowland hundred) which, legend claims, now lies beneath the waves of Cardigan Bay.

Thomas Love Peacock, the 19th century poet and novelist, told of Seithenyn's blinkered stupidity in 'The Misfortunes of Elphin', a tale involving several figures from Welsh legend. When Prince Elphin sought out the foolish man and told him of reports about the dangerous, decayed state of the sea defences, Seithenyn scorned the criticism; he had heard it all before. "That is the beauty of it, some parts of it are rotten and some parts of it are sound," was his reply. Elphin suggested it would be better for everyone who lived in Cantref y Gwaelod if all the walls, embankments, flood-gates and sluices were maintained in the best possible condition. Seithenyn scoffed at such a perverse suggestion which could have come only from people "blind to venerable antiquity".

"The parts that are rotten give elasticity to those that are sound" was his self-satisfied response. Then he added, "If it were all sound, it would break by its own obstinate stiffness; the soundness is checked by the rottenness and the stiffness is balanced by the elasticity. There is nothing so dangerous as innovation." Seithenyn refilled his cup with wine and continued, "This immortal old work has stood for centuries, and will stand for centuries more, if we let well alone. It is well: it works well: let well alone. It was half rotten when I was born, and that is a conclusive reason why it should be three parts rotten when I die."

Disaster was not long delayed. One night Seithenyn drank himself into a stupor, neglected to shut the leaky, creaky flood-gates and an equinoctial storm, whipped up by gale-force winds, sent huge waves roaring and pouring, dashing and clashing, spattering and battering, rattling and battling against the weakened defences. With tempestuous fury the waters exacted terrible retribution for Seithenyn's myopic folly on the innocent inhabitants of the lowlands. The sea flooded in drowning people, horses, cattle and sheep; King Gwyddno Garanhir's court of Caer Wyddno vanished for ever beneath the waves, as did 16 of the finest fortified towns of Wales. Some say that only one man escaped the devastation by mounting his horse and just keeping ahead of the advancing flood-tide in a hair-raising, headlong gallop to safety. He lived out his remaining years haunted by the terror of that fateful night. Others say that there were more survivors who struggled out of the mud and debris onto a new shoreline when the storm eventually abated. These refugees from a vanished land made new homes in Arfon, Ardudwy and other uninhabited places amid Snowdonia's mountains. Evidence of the disaster, which is said to have occurred 16 centuries ago (although in reality it probably happened in Neolithic times), are ancient tree stumps revealed by low tides on beaches near Borth and the 'causeways' which lead to the lost land such as Sarn Gynfelyn at Wallog near Aberystwyth, Sarn Badrig (St Patrick's Causeway) which runs south-westward for several miles from the coast near Llanbedr, and others near Aberarth. More lost forests are indicated by tree stumps revealed by scouring tides at Amroth, Marros and Newgale.

Another vanished province was Tyno Helig in Conwy Bay, the domain of Helig ap Glannog, the claimed father of several Welsh saints. Cadwallon, a 7th century King of Gwynedd, was besieged on Priestholm (Ynys Seiriol) by Edwin of Northumbria's Saxon army but before the island became an embattled, water-girt haven for warriors or the tiny island home of monks, legend says it was a hill of Helig's flat and fruitful land whose shoreline stretched from Priestholm to Great Ormes Head and included the area covered by the Lavan Sands.

Again inundation came as retribution – not to punish human neglect and foolishness, but as atonement for the proud and worldly ways of Helig's court. Many times during a night long ago servants had replenished the drinking-horns with wine as Helig and his warrior-captains caroused, relived and retold tales of their prowess at arms. The dark, winter evening hours passed in merriment, laughter, cheers and crash of fists on food-laden tables. At last the palace fell silent, but Helig's sleep was disturbed by terrifying nightmares. He woke, his skin damp with the sweat of fear and cries stifled in his throat. He threw a robe over his shoulders, grasped a sword and as he stalked the stilled, moonlight-splashed corridors he felt the cold grip of terror tighten again. He heard a whisper – or was it but the dying sigh of the wind? He turned and stabbed with his sword; its point pierced only air and shadow. The whisper came again. Once more he slashed but the blade's stone-honed edge cut through nought but silver-grey moonlight. Silence. The whisper came again. It grew into a soft but insistent moan. Helig retreated but the ghostly voice pursued him. He cowered in a corner and the sword-hilt fell from his fingers. "Vengeance will come! Vengeance will come!" Stronger, louder, the words reverberated and resounded around the halls but no-one heard them but Helig.

Helig's fears waned as the light and bustle of a new day invaded his palace but the ghostly warning voice echoed in his brain. For hours he sat silent and motionless, then he ran to the stables, mounted his horse and galloped eastward towards the mountains. His mount panted clouds of steam when he reached his goal – the remote turf-roofed hut of an old hermit who had the gift of foreseeing the future. Helig nervously recounted his night of terror, the dreadful nightmare and the warnings whispered by an invisible spirit. "What does it mean?" he asked, his voice filled with foreboding. The old seer prophesied that the lowlands would be destroyed and pointing a finger at Helig he added, "It will be in the time of thy grandchildren, thy great-grandchildren and their children". A smile of relief broadened across Helig's face as he realised the threat would not be fulfilled for another three generations.

Time slowly erased the memory of whispered ghostly warnings and Helig grew old in the comfort and wealth of his domain. Years passed, his sons gave him grandchildren and they in their turn fathered a new generation. One day the family of old Helig gathered at Llys Helig to celebrate a new birth – all were there even unto the new-born fifth generation. The sounds of laughter and merrymaking rang through the halls. Jugs of wine were emptied and replenished and a servant hurried to the cellar in answer to the shouts of "More wine! More wine!" As he descended the stairs he saw water pouring through the walls and rising fast. His blurted warning was ignored by everyone except Helig into whose mind flashed the memory of a long-forgotten night of terror and an old man's prophecy. As Helig rose from his seat an expectant hush was broken by a distant noise like the far-off rumble of thunder. The drumming grew louder, drowning all human cries in a crashing crescendo as a giant wave burst through the door and windows.

In the 17th century Sir John Wynn of Gwydir wrote that the remains of Helig's court were sometimes revealed by low tides – 'the ruines (of Llys Helig) whereof is nowe to bee seene uppon a grownd ebbe some two myles within the sea directly over against Trefyn yr Wylfa, unto which hill Helyg ap Glannog and his people did run upp to save theyselves, being endaungered with the sudden breakynge in of the sea upon them, and there saved their lyves.' He claimed that there were the remains of a causeway across the strait from Priestholm, which he attributed to St Seiriol, founder of Penmon Church, Anglesey, and its cell on the little island which bears his name. The 'pavement' was laid so that the saint could 'walk dry' from his hermitage isle to a chapel at Penmaenmawr. Women were not allowed to set foot on Priestholm and when the island's hermit monks quarrelled amongst themselves their unholy behaviour was punished by a plague of mice which ate their food until they stopped.

Legend says that another drowned land of large extent lies under the sea of Caernarfon Bay between the north coast of Lleyn and Anglesey. When King Bran of the 'Island of the Mighty' (one of the bardic names for Britain) led his army from Caernarfon to Ireland to avenge the wrong done to his sister Branwen, his troops made the voyage in ships but the king, a giant of a man, walked all the way. That was how the invasion was described in an ancient tale which said that long ago the sea between Wales and Ireland was not very wide. Bran could wade his way to Ireland because, so says the story, the coastal lowlands of western Wales had not been inundated by the ocean. A few miles from Caernarfon are the beachside remains of the Iron Age fort of Dinas Dinlle whose seaward side is being eroded by the sea. The site is mentioned in 'Math, son of Mathonwy' another Mabinogion story, as is the tiny islet of Caer Arianrhod which is now more than half a mile from the beach about a mile south of Dinas Dinlle. The islet which, in the story, travellers could approach on foot from the east but by ship from the west, was the home of the deceitful Aranrhod. Her lies were discovered when, to test her claim of virginity, she stepped over a magic wand and instantly gave birth to two sons, one of whom, Dylan, gave his name to the headland of Trwyn Maen Dylan a mile south of Caer Arianrhod. Legend also claims that somewhere in that submerged land are the remains of a Roman fort.

The sea is prominent in many Welsh folktales, and it has been a major influence on the history of the principality and its people. Rocks and treacherous currents around rugged coasts have claimed many victims – St Asaph Cathedral has an ivory Madonna said to have come from a wrecked Spanish Armada galleon. Norse pirates raided in search of plunder and, in one instance, kidnapped Iago ap Idwal, Prince of Gwynedd, who then vanished from history. A more famous victim of pirates was St Patrick who was carried off as a slave to Ireland and the name of Ireland's patron saint (legend claims it was he who expelled serpents from that island) is incorporated in that of the tiny Anglesey community of Llanbadrig whose church he is said to have founded in thanksgiving for escaping shipwreck. The cliffside church – "In certain winds the waves break over it with such violence as to interrupt and prevent the performance of divine service" wrote a traveller – is between symbols of civilisations ancient and modern – to the east is Dinas Gynfor, an Iron Age promontory fort, and to the west across Cemaes Bay a nuclear power station. In the 19th century Llanbadrig Church was restored by the eccentric Lord Stanley of Alderley, who, being a Muslim, ordered Islamic features to be incorporated into the work. Lord Stanley wedded his lady-love four times by various rites and was then much galled to discover that she already had a husband.

Other maritime tragedies remembered along the Anglesey coast include the destruction in 1859 of the 'Royal Charter'. Bound for Liverpool with passengers, wool, golden sovereigns and gold ingots from Australia, the ship broke into three parts during an October gale off Moelfre and more than 450 people drowned. Charles Dickens travelled to the little church at Llanallgo which became a mortuary for the scores of bodies awaiting burial in local churchyards. The novelist described the sad aftermath of the wreck in one of the episodes of 'The Uncommercial Traveller'. He told how a man living on a hill-top overlooking the sea was blown out of bed by the wind which was stripping his roof. As he climbed onto the top of his house to make repairs he saw "as he looked down by chance towards the shore, some dark troubled object close in with the land."

Dickens described the impotence of would-be rescuers standing on the shore – "And so, over the hill-slopes, and past the waterfall, and down the gullies where the land drains off into the ocean, the scattered quarrymen and fishermen inhabiting that part of Wales had come running to the dismal sight – their clergyman among them. And as they stood in the leaden morning, stricken with pity, leaning hard against the wind, their breath and vision often failing as the sleet and spray rushed at them from the ever forming and dissolving mountains of sea, and as

Llangorse Lake where murder and a queen's greed brought stormy retribution. Now it is a centre for water sports.

the wool which was a part of the vessel's cargo blew in with the salt foam and remained upon the land when the foam melted, they saw the ship's life-boat put off from one of the heaps of wreck; and first, there were three men in her, and in a moment she capsized, and there were but two; and again, she was struck by a vast mass of water, and there was but one; and again, she was thrown bottom upward, and that one, with his arm struck through the broken planks and waving as if for the help that could never reach him, went down into the deep." In the days before organised emergency services it was left largely to the local community to deal with catastrophes and the parson of Llanallgo, the Rev Stephen Hughes, whose brother was vicar of two neighbouring parishes, wrote more than a thousand letters to relatives and friends of the victims.

A century earlier on the other side of the island, Rhosneigr had had an evil reputation as being the nest of a gang of shipwreckers who operated along the coast. They had been hunted down and hanged in 1741. Their story was told by the poet Lewis Morris who has a memorial not far from the scene of the 'Royal Charter' tragedy. But the people of Llanallgo, Lligwy and Moelfre made no profit from the wreck. All the handymen of the neighbourhood helped with making coffins and Dickens noted, "The people were none the richer for the wreck, for it was the season of the herring-shoal – and who could cast nets for fish, and find dead men and women in the draughts?"

Eighty years after the destruction of the passsenger ship the seas near Llanallgo claimed almost a hundred more lives when the submarine 'Thetis' failed to surface during trials in the bay off Traeth Bychan. Even more recently there have been mysterious tragedies off the Welsh coast when small fishing vessels and some of their crews have vanished – instances blamed by some on submarine activity in the Irish Sea.

According to legend, earlier generations of fishermen had encoun-tered creatures from beneath the waves of the Irish Sea. Some fishermen sailed out into Cardigan Bay one day and cast their nets into the sea. When they hauled in the nets they were amazed to find a mermaid helplessly entangled in the mesh. The tearful sea-maiden pleaded with the crew to release her, promising to give them three timely warnings "when you shall need them most". The sailors carefully freed the frightened creature and the mermaid joyfully slid over the side of the boat and disappeared beneath the waves. Weeks became months and the fishermen neither heard nor saw any sign of the mermaid as they sailed across the bay in search of a catch. But the mermaid was true to her promise. It had seemed a perfect day for fishing as the crew of the little boat ran out their nets in the company of a flotilla of other craft. The sea was as calm as a millpond and only a gentle breeze fluttered the rigging beneath a cloudless sky. Suddenly the mermaid appeared alongside the boat. "Haul in your nets," she cried. The sailors smiled and continued their work. Again, and with more urgency, the voice cried to them to retrieve their nets. The fishermen looked at one another – what should they do? The mermaid swam close to the gunwale and in a tone more commanding than entreating, she called on them to haul in their nets. This time the fishermen obeyed and to the accompaniment of derisory shouts from other boats, they raised their sail and steered towards the shore. Even as they entered harbour the wind was whipping up foam-topped rollers taller than a man, and out to sea grey-black clouds darkened the sky. The storm howled and battered throughout the night and when a new day dawned calm and clear there were pieces of smashed driftwood along the strand and many a new widow and orphan in the little village of fisherfolk.

According to another story the fishermen of Conwy showed no such pity when they encountered a mermaid. Many centuries before King Edward I built his towering castle there, a storm whipped up the sea in Conwy Bay and a mermaid was swept onto the shore. The beached sea creature, bruised and exhausted, pleaded with some fishermen to carry her into the water. The hard-hearted fishermen ignored her cries and as she grew weaker she shouted a curse on them and their town – "Long shall ye toil and never shall ye prosper." Down the generations whenever a Conwy boat returned with little in its hold the curse was blamed.

Across the estuary from Conwy are the remains of Deganwy Castle, a fortress with a bloody history of conflict. Long before invading Normans built their castle on the site it was the court of Maelgwyn Gwynedd, a sixth century king who is the subject of many old tales. It is said that Maelgwyn acquired his kingdom with a notable piece of cunning. To decide which of several claimants should wear the crown a contest was held on the sands of the Dovey estuary. There the candidates had to sit on chairs and he that defied the incoming tide longest would be declared king. When the others retreated to safety as the water reached their lips Maelgwyn smiled, the water still not over his ankles. Maelgwyn had studied the rules and found that it was not so much what they said as what they did not say. He had instructed his carpenter to build him a special chair for the contest, one which would gently rise on the flood-tide. And in commemoration of his success the sands of the Dovey estuary are still called Traeth Maelgwyn.

Echoing tales from other regions is the story of his queen's ring. One day Maelgwyn's wife was bathing in the clear waters of a mountain pool from which a stream tumbled down the hillside to the river Elwy in the valley below. It was not until she returned to Deganwy that she realised that the precious ruby ring worn by every Queen of Gwynedd had slipped off her finger. Fearing her husband's anger at her carelessness, she hastened to tell her tale to St Asaph, the abbot of the cathedral monastery in the little town that bears his name. The holy man smiled, said that he would explain the mishap to the king and all would be well. He also invited the king and queen to be his guests in the refectory for a celebratory banquet on the feast day of the cathedral's founder, St Kentigern. Abbot Asaph spoke of the queen's accidental loss of the ring and Maelgwyn's face frowned in anger as a servant placed a golden platter bearing a huge salmon in front of him. "This magnificent fish was

49

The Teifi at Cenarth Falls – when Gerald of Wales came this way in 1188 salmon leapt and beavers were busy.

netted only this morning at the weir below the cathedral," said Asaph, his eyes gleaming in expectation. As Melgwyn cut into the fish he felt his knife strike something hard. There in the belly of the fish lay the lost ring – the king's anger evaporated, the queen's joy caused her to endow the monastery with a rich gift, and Asaph said a silent prayer of thanks with his eyes gazing upward towards the stars. A similar fishy tale is associated with St Kentigern, the claimed founder of a monastery at St Asaph in the mid-sixth century. The monk Kentigern (also known as Mungo) spent much of his life spreading the Christian faith in Strathclyde. The tale is told that there the queen had given her ring to her lover. When the king discovered the illicit liaison, he took the ring and threw it into the sea, and then told his wife to produce it within three days. The worried queen sought Kentigern's aid and the saint duly produced the ring from the belly of a freshly caught salmon.

The chronicler monk Gildas said Maelgwyn's court at Deganwy was an ungodly and licentious place, and retribution came when yellow plague struck the region. Maelgwyn sought sanctuary in the little church at Llanrhos below the hill which still carries his name. While pestilence raged outside he refused to open the door to anyone until one day, so legend says, he peeped through a hole, saw the plague manifest itself in the form of a monster and he expired of fright in the year 547 (when Asaph and Kentigern were still boys). A man who, unlike King Cnut, was successful in defying the tide was St Illtud. When the sea threatened to inundate his lands in Gower an angel appeared and told him to defiantly raise his staff and, in a loud voice, order the tide to retreat. This he did and the waves rolled back from the land and when he lowered his staff a well of fresh water burst forth where it touched the earth.

One of Maelgwyn's successors, Gruffydd ap Llywelyn, who ruled much of Wales and inflicted defeats on the English, escaped by ship when Earl Harold (later King of England) attacked his fort at Rhuddlan. Harold returned and Gruffydd was murdered by his own men and his head was delivered to the earl who later married the Welsh ruler's widow. Vikings plundered coastal monasteries and legend claims that Prince Madog of Gwynedd set out with 10 ships and 300 men – perhaps from Porthmadog – on a one-way voyage across the Atlantic long before Christopher Columbus discovered the 'New World'. Some say the Mandan tribe of the North American great plains were the descendants of his Welsh-speaking crew.

Other Welsh seamen found fame (or evil notoriety) and fortune across the seas. Henry Morgan was a famous buccaneer who enjoyed royal favour. In 1671 he sacked Panama, the richest town in Spain's American empire, gained a knighthood from Charles II and was made governor of Jamaica. The distinction between buccaneer, privateer and pirate was a fine one but two Welshmen who revelled in outright piratical exploits were Howell Davis and Bartholomew Roberts, two of the most feared sea rovers of the early 18th century. The fatefully brief acquaintance of the two men began when Davis attacked a slave port on the Guinea coast in

1719. Roberts, who was born in Little Newcastle, was one of a slaveship crew taken aboard the pirate captain's ship, 'Royal Rover'. A few weeks later Howell Davis was dead, killed in an ambush during an attack on a Portuguese settlement, and Roberts, an expert seaman, was elected to command by the 'company of wild ungovernable brutes' as Daniel Defoe described the pirate crew. For the next three years Roberts made the name of Black Bart the scourge of the oceans from the Caribbean to Africa. Toting four pistols and a cutlass, he flew two black flags from his masts – one depicted him drinking with a skeleton, the other showed him brandishing a sword and standing on two skulls.

Roberts' violent end came in African waters in 1722 when his squadron of three ships encountered the Royal Navy's 60-gun 'Swallow'. Roberts tried to fight it out and was killed by the first broadside, his throat torn out by grape-shot. His body, dressed in pirate captain's finery, was thrown overboard and the pirate survivors were taken to Cape Coast Castle where many of them were hanged in the African sun – "Ye and each of you are adjudged and sentenced to be carried back to the place from whence ye came, from thence to the place of Execution without the Galow of this Castle; and there within the Flood Marks to be Hanged by the Neck 'till ye are Dead, Dead, Dead and the Lord have Mercy on your souls."

Much of Black Bart's loot came from ransoming his captures. The elusive John Paul Jones, who despite his name was an emigrant son of a Scottish gardener, sailed into Fishguard Bay during America's War of Independence, seized a merchantman and demanded a ransom. When golden guineas failed to materialise he fired a broadside into the town and departed. A couple of decades later three other foreign men o'war anchored off Fishguard in a farcical episode of military ineptitude. Britain was at war with France and on February 22, 1797, some 1,400 men, mostly convicts, led by an Irish-American general attempted the last 'invasion' of Britain. They came ashore from three frigates near Strumble Head and for many of them the first priority was to get their hands on any available booze. After a couple of days in which the people of west Wales showed that they had no inclination to rise in revolution, as the misguided French had expected them to, the invaders, many of them drunk, were rounded up without bloodshed by the militia. Surrender was signed at Fishguard's Royal Oak inn. It is said the French lost what little stomach they had for a fight when they mistook the red cloaks of local ladies who had gathered as curious spectators for soldiers' redcoats. One no-nonsense local female, 'a tall stout Amazon masculine woman who worked as a cobbler' was Jemima Nicholas (her memorial is in the church) who marched in a dozen invaders at the point of a pitchfork.

Five centuries earlier command of the sea had been vital in the wars of conquest waged by King Edward I against Llywelyn ap Gruffydd (Llywelyn the Last) of Gwynedd, and the castles built by the English king at Flint, Rhuddlan, Conwy, Caernarfon, Harlech and Beaumaris could all be supplied and reinforced by ships. In later ages smugglers conducted their illicit but popular trade on deserted beaches and one enterprising and quick-witted gang escaped the close attention of revenue officers by protesting that the spiritual potency of the liquid contained in the casks they were heaving along the sand was confined to its health-giving properties because it was merely clear, pure water drawn from a nearby holy well. Jocular tales of rustics finding smuggled rum and waking with a hangover unable to remember where they had hidden the spirit are common.

Sea water was not the only means of reprisal on the wicked in ancient times. As well as towns and fruitful lands lost to salty tides, there were the courts of the sinful hidden forever beneath mountain lakes. A few miles east of Brecon is Llangorse Lake whose waters, they say, blot out a city as punishment for greed and murder. Here ruled a beautiful queen who delighted in luxury and villainy. Many warriors displayed their prowess in attempts to win her favour but the dark-haired beauty had little interest in skill at arms. She wanted gold and jewels and fine silks. One day, while hunting, she noted with silent satisfaction how a low-born groom looked upon her with eyes filled with longing.

During the ensuing weeks she deliberately inflamed the passion he could not disguise, then, one day, she whispered, "I can be yours – for seven sacks of gold!" The ostler brooded on the queen's words. How could he get his hands on so much money? The city square thronged with men and women, buyers and sellers, rich and poor during May fair week and the groom noted how one merchant filled and refilled his purse with coins from the sale of his wares. The night sky was clear, no cloud obscured the moon's face, as the foolish trader slowly made his way over the Black Mountains towards Hereford. On a lonely mountainside an assassin struck without warning. A blade glinted in the silver moonlight for a split-second before it was buried to its hilt in the fat merchant's chest. The body was rolled into a ravine and a shower of stones was sent tumbling down the cliff to cover the corpse. Strapped to the packhorse were seven bulging sacks, each filled with coins of gold.

The queen offered her hand to the peasant's son who, to her wide-eyed delight, proudly displayed seven piles of gold. As queen and consort lay together that night in the royal bedchamber, they heard the distant deep toll of bells from Llanthony Priory borne across the mountains by an east wind. Then the bloodied white spectre of the merchant floated before them – "Vengeance, vengeance shall come! I shall be avenged! The stain of murder shall be washed away at the seventh generation when a seventh son shall beget a seventh son." But like Helig, they soon forgot the warning. Years passed and new generations were born even down to the seventh generation. A great-great-great-grandson sired seven sons and the seventh son was already the father of six boys when the midwives closseted his wife again. The old queen, her beauty long since vanished, heard the slap and cry of a new-born child – "It's a boy!" came the cry. Instantly there was a flash of lightning and a crack of thunder over Mynydd Llangorse and from the heavens came huge teardrops of rain. The storm hung over Llangorse for seven days and seven nights, torrents of water rushed down the mountain until palace, houses, shops and churches had vanished. Some say there was a single survivor, a child not more than a week old, swaddled in a wicker cradle which gently rode the flood, but whether he was the seventh son of a seventh son no-one ever knew.

Near Oswestry there are many relics of vanished generations. Wat's Dyke and Offa's Dyke once marked Saxon England's border, Old Oswestry and Llanmynech Hill were tribal forts, and there are the remains of several castles. The town's name recalls St Oswald, a king of Northumbria who was defeated in battle and crucified (hence Oswald's Tree) by Penda of Mercia in 642. Also near Oswestry is Llyn Llynclys which is associated in legend with another tale of feminine vanity and masculine passion. Centuries ago a king of the region was growing old but still he had an eye for beauty. One day, while hunting in the forest, he encountered a veritable Venus who flattered and charmed him. The radiant maiden was also forward. "Take me as your queen, sire, and my young body shall warm you through the cold nights of winter," she said. Then she added, "However, you must give your word that each seventh night I may go whither I choose and you shall never ask me whence I go." Blinded by desire the old king agreed and turned his horse's head towards the palace, eager to order his old wife to a nunnery. But of his stooping, white-haired spouse of many years there was no sign, indeed he never laid eyes on her again.

Like the magician Merlin when tempted by Vivien, the king had no shield against the seductive enchantments of a young beauty. He revelled in her coquettish attentions but each seventh night, when she left him to sleep alone, the seed of suspicion blossomed. The king confided his fears in Willin, a monk who secretly dabbled in alchemy and the black arts and who, for many months, had been consulting the ancient books for spells which would make the 'maid of the green forest' his own. At last, it seemed, his unbridled desire would be satisfied. Another week passed and Willin stealthily followed the young queen along lonely forest paths to a cave. He paused at the entrance, rehearsing the words of a spell which would make her look fondly upon him, and another which, despite the passing years, would keep her forever young and beautiful. "No change let her form betide," he incanted as he entered the cleft in the rock, his heart pounding in eager anticipation. But the monk found no nymph to make his fantasies of love come true. He beheld a bent-backed, leather-faced crone. He cringed in disgust and amazement; it was the king's old wife. Instantly the truth was apparent. She had made a pact with the Devil – she had sold her soul as the price of regularly rejuvenated beauty. Retribution was swift. King, court and palace were swallowed by the lake while the monk was condemned to pass bitter eternity in the company of a boney-fingered hag whose form, thanks to his own spells, would never change.

The original sites of other towns such as Mathry and Tregaron in

Llyn Ogwen – from its clear waters a hand emerged to take back King Arthur's sword Excalibur.

Dyfed are said to be covered by lakes. Llyn Tegid (Bala Lake) covers an old town too; disaster came when a forgetful woman failed to replace the cover on the town well which overflowed during the night. Llyn Lech Owain near Llandeilo formed when a legendary hero who hid from his enemies on Mynydd Mawr watered his horse at a spring and neglected to put back the covering stone. The flood might have been worse but Owain used his magic powers to limit the overflow to a small mountain lake. Now he, like King Arthur, sleeps in a cave awaiting the trumpet call to new battles while the lake ensures that his name is never forgotten. Near the Lleyn village of Llangybi, famed for St Cybi's holy well, is Llyn Glasfryn. Here, they say, the wind carries the remorseful wails of the negligent woman who allowed a holy well to overflow. Not only can she sometimes be heard, but nearby is a standing stone which some say is the petrified culprit condemned to stand forever as a reminder to others.

When the Devil planned to bring watery destruction to the people of the villages along the Teifi by damming the river, he was tricked into giving up his scheme by a quick-thinking shoemaker who was making his way home to Llandyssul one night. The shoemaker saw the Devil coming towards him with a huge shovelful of earth. "How far is the river?" the Devil demanded. Guessing what was planned the cobbler brandished a bundle of old shoes, their soles full of holes, and replied, "Many miles, see, I have already worn these out on the journey." Disheartened, the Devil tipped the soil and rock off his spade and departed. Many folktales are associated with mountain lakes of Wales. Some tell of human encounters with monsters and fairy folk, others record restless hauntings by spectres of the dead. High in the mountains, near the source of the river Usk, are two lakes. Long ago it was recorded that while the smaller one teemed with fish, the larger Llyn y Fan Fawr had none at all and that if fish were put into it they turned belly-up and died as soon as they tasted its waters. But it was not an abundance of fish life which made Llyn y Fan Fach, the smaller of the two lakes, notable in Welsh legend.

One day a young shepherd was resting beside the lake when he saw a wondrous sight. Sitting on the waters of the lake was a beautiful maiden slowly brushing her long fair hair. Instantly the shepherd fell in love but despite all his entreaties the maiden would neither approach nor speak to him. Day after day he returned to Llyn y Fan Fach hoping to see his beloved, and when he did he would offer her gifts as proof of his devotion but the maid was steadfast in ignoring him. Eventually, however, the young man's tireless suit was rewarded when, one day in high summer, she accepted some bread. "Return tomorrow and the marriage pact shall be made," she said with a smile and then disappeared. On the morrow the shepherd waited impatiently on the bank until, as the evening sun began to glow red and drop towards the horizon, he saw an old man appear out of the lake holding the hands of two beautiful women. As the trio glided across the water the old man spoke, "Young man, my daughter shall be thy wife, if ye can tell which is she to whom ye have declared thy undying love and which is her sister."

The shepherd looked intently into the faces of the two women and his heart sank as he realised that they were twins in every respect – eyes, hair, hands, even the gowns and robes they wore were identical. "Speak, which is she whom ye love?" demanded the old man. The puzzled shepherd did not know which to choose. As he turned his head away in despair he noticed a breadcrumb lodged in the fastening of one of the girls' shoes. Overjoyed, he turned towards the father and cried triumphantly, "It is she whom you hold with your right hand!"

"Ye have chosen true, she shall be thy wife and together shall ye prosper. However, know this, should ye strike her, be it yet soft and innocent, at the third needless blow thy marriage shall end and never again shall ye behold the daughter I now give unto thee." The father's prediction of prosperity soon came true because as the shepherd walked down the mountain with his bride, out of the lake there appeared five times five of the finest sheep the young man had ever seen, then five times five goats, then milch cows and horses. The shepherd and his fairy wife lived together joyfully. They raised a family of healthy sons and thanks to the dowry of a hundred animals, their wealth increased with each passing year. One day they made ready to go to church for their youngest son's christening and when the wife hesitated the husband chided her and gave her a gentle nudge. When their eldest son was married the wife gave way to tears and her husband patted her cheek saying it was unseemly behaviour for such a day. After each incident the wife warned her spouse that a causeless blow had been struck.

The husband, mindful of the old man's warning, was exceedingly careful until the day of a neighbour's funeral. The solemn husband misinterpreted his wife's smiles as disrespect and grasped her wrist as though to shake her. Tears welled in her eyes as she spoke, "Husband, thrice have you rebuked me and laid your hands upon me without just cause. I must now return whence I came." The prosperous shepherd watched in silence with his sons as she climbed the mountain towards Llyn y Fan Fach with all the sheep and goats, horses and catttle of the farm, the offspring of the fairy dowry, following in her footsteps. The husband had to sell the farm and take the job of a shepherd. Often he stared into the waters of Llyn y Fan Fach in hope of glimpsing his wife but never was it to be. His three sons, however, did see their mother again. She would appear to them as they sat at the lakeside and instruct them in the magic of herbs and wild flowers. They learned well and the knowledge she imparted caused them to become the most famous physicians in the land. Kings, princes and nobles gave purses of gold when they sought the healers' advice, but from the poor the three brother doctors of Myddfai asked no payment.

In Snowdonia Llyn Ogwen is said to be the lake from which an arm appeared to take back King Arthur's sword, Excalibur, whereas the black water of Llyn Dulyn was home to ugly, huge-headed fish. Here too, was a rock, 'the red altar', at the end of a causeway, which, when splashed with clear water, would invariably grant a wish for rain before midnight. Now

Llyn Dulyn is a reservoir and its 'magic' has been exorcised. Llyn-y-dywarchen had a floating island held together by roots upon which, according to the 12th century priest and writer Gerald of Wales, unwary animals would be wafted by the breeze across the lake on unexpected voyages. Legend claims that Llyn Idwal preserves the name of a prince of Gwynedd who was cruelly murdered by his foster-father. While Idwal's spirit haunts the environs of the lake, that of his killer is condemned to an eternity without rest stalking Twll Du (the Devil's Kitchen). Cadair Idris (Chair of Idris) is haunted by a spirit which can assume human form and has the power to call down storms and impenetrable mists. When storms and mists clear the demon collects the bodies of his victims and dumps them in a mountain lake.

From the Conwy Valley comes the tale of a monster whose activities often resulted in floods. The long-suffering people of the area decided that the afanc (literally beaver) had to go. Their first tactic was to try to drive the huge beast away by force but their spears and arrows could not penetrate its hairy exterior. Then a new and more cunning plan was devised. The loveliest maid in the Vale of Conwy sat beside the river combing her hair and singing a soothing lullaby. The afanc emerged, laid its head on the girl's lap and contentedly went to sleep. When the signal was given, five blacksmiths appeared from behind the rocks and attached specially forged chains to the beast's legs and neck. With a bellow the animal awoke and tried to run to its lair in the river but the chains held and the afanc fell exhausted to the ground. Then appeared the valley farmers with their teams of oxen to drag the monster high into the mountains where it was released into the lonely blue waters of Glaslyn. Another monster of legend was killed in Dyfed and its grave is said to be Bedd-yr-Afanc, a prehistoric tomb near Brynberian.

In the hills above the estuary of the river Dovey is Llyn Barfog (the Bearded Lake) which is associated with a tale with echoes of that of the shepherd who married the fairy bride of Llyn y Fan Fach. One day a poor, hard-working farmer had a stroke of good fortune when a magical white cow strayed from the lake, the home of green-clad fairy maidens. The cow produced milk in superabundance and the sale of cheese and butter made the farmer wealthy, particularly when its numerous offspring did likewise. But when the cow grew old the ungrateful miser, who had grown indolent in his comfort, saw the chance of extra profit by slaughtering the benevolent beast for meat. His meanness was avenged. As the butcher lifted his axe to despatch the cow a fearful cry echoed from the hills around the lake and the old cow and its progeny cantered off to disappear beneath the waters of Llyn Barfog. Soon the farmer's wealth dwindled and he was again reduced to poverty. Perhaps the poor man had the consolation of hearing the music of the bells of Seithenyn's lost lowlands. As in the enduring tales of Dunwich and elsewhere, it is said the churchbells of Cantref y Gwaelod can be heard tolling beneath the waves. Others say that the music of the submerged bells can be heard only by true lovers, or, as in the words of an old song – "If to me as true thou art, as I am true to thee sweetheart, we'll hear one, two, three, four, five from the bells of Aberdovey."

Two miles east of Ffestiniog is Llyn Morwynion (Lake of the Maidens) from which appear the spirits of virgins to comb their tresses in the first light of dawn. These maidens died for love. The story is that long ago the men of Ardudwy, an area rich in prehistoric remains between Harlech and Barmouth, made a foray into the Vale of Clwyd in search of wives. The raiders and their willing captives dallied in the mountains on the way back and a posse of understandably incensed fathers and fiances of Clwyd caught up with them near the lake. A battle ensued in which the men of Ardudwy were slain whereupon the grief-stricken maidens committed suicide by jumping into the lake.

An alternative tale, told in the Mabinogion, says that the maidens were from Blodeuedd's court at Tomen-y-Mur, a Roman military base in wild moorland above Llyn Trawsfynydd. The fort has a small amphitheatre and a castle mound dating from the Norman invasions of Gwynedd. Blodeuedd was the magically created wife of Lleu Llaw Gyffes, one of the sons 'dropped' by Aranrhod when she stepped over a magic wand. When Blodeuedd and her lover tried to kill Lleu he became an eagle which the magician Gwydion restored to human form. Blodeuedd and her maidens fled across the river Cynfal when she saw Lleu's avenging army coming but in their terror-stricken flight they did not look where they were going and fell into the lake and all except Blodeuedd drowned. Gwydion turned her into an owl.

A few miles eastward of this scene of legendary self-destruction and magical transformation are examples of how the work of man and nature have changed the coastline of Wales. A broad estuary, Traeth Mawr, was reclaimed in the early 19th century when a mile long embankment which carries the Ffestiniog Railway and a road was built across the river Glaslyn at Porthmadog. South of The Cob (embankment), across Traeth Bach from the Italianate village of Porthmeirion, the little church and hamlet of Llanfihangel-y-traethau (St. Michael's in the estuary) stand above the surrounding lowlands and sands. A tombstone says the original church was built during the 12th century reign of Owain Gwynedd, at which time Llanfihangel was a tidal island. On the north coast, in the churchyard of another church dedicated to St Michael at Abergele, an old tombstone recorded the death of a man whose home was three miles to the north – a point now more than two miles out to sea. Advancing sands brought ruin to the borough and castle of Kenfig which the Normans had founded in the 12th century, and at Goldcliff beside the Severn a brass in the church records another of the innumerable watery tragedies, great and small, which have befallen Wales – '1606 on the xx day of January, even as it came to pas it pleased God the flud did flow to the edge of this same bras and in this parish theare was lost 5000 and od pownds besides, xxii people was in this parish drownd.' More memorials to the great 1606 flood – 'the worst since Noah' – are in other churches in this low-lying region.

Holy hermits, miracles, magic of the wells and love and curses

Wherever you go in Wales there are reminders never very far away that saints and holy men have preceded you. It may be a cathedral, church or chapel in city, town or village. It may be a tiny church isolated high in the mountains or perched close to the sea. The name of town or village may incorporate the memory of an obscure holy hermit whose cult was strictly local or one whose renown stretched throughout Christendom. A natural feature of the landscape bearing a saint's name (St Non's Bay, St Tudwal's Islands, St Govan's Head) or the ancient ruins of a monastery may recall an old story. It could be a holy well, one of the hundreds which dotted the countryside and which, in centuries long ago, would have been a centre for local religious ritual or, perchance, one whose fame and reputed healing qualities caused pilgrims, be they kings or peasants, to travel many a mile.

Many wells were said to have healing properties and for the supplicant, who usually made an offering of pins, buttons or coins, it was a matter of matching the ailment with the well, such was their claimed collective ability to treat virtually every human ill. The rituals varied from straightforward drinking or bathing in the water to complex ceremonies involving the recitation of prayers or sleeping on a tomb. Some wells, it was believed, could divine a lover's constancy, others could effect a curse – that at Llanelian-yn-Rhos had a most sinister reputation. For a fee the future fortune of a rival or enemy could be thoroughly blighted, although for a considerably higher charge the malediction could be just as promptly lifted. Such unscrupulous enterprise in an age of superstition proved highly profitable!

Dozens of saints, some of them of suspect provenance, are remembered in scores of place names. Llanfair is among the commonest and recalls St Mary; Llanfihangel denotes St Michael's church (Llanfihangel-yng-Ngwynfa high in the mountains of Powys is the delightfully named St Michael's in Paradise); Llanbedr incorporates the name of the disciple St Peter, and Llanddewi tells of a dedication to Wales' patron, St David. To distinguish his Anglesey Llanfair from all others, a 19th century tradesman concocted Llanfairpwllgwyngyllgogery-chwyrndrobwllllantysiliogogogoch with an eye to enhancing the village cash-flow from tourism. He tacked on details of the local scenery and worked in another saint's name as well to make it mean in translation – 'St Mary's church in a hollow by the white hazel near the rapid whirlpool by St Tysilio's red cave'. Llanfair P.G's. other claim to fame is that it was home to the first Women's Institute founded in 1915. Tysilio's activities were centred in Powys (Llandyssilio) but perhaps he did shelter in a cave when he founded a small chapel close by on an islet in the Menai Strait. The seventh century chapel has been replaced by a small medieval church, now reached by a causeway. Among documented saints are

*St Brynach's Cross in Nevern churchyard from which
the first cuckoo announced the arrival of Spring.*

Cadfan of Llangadfan, Cadwaladr of Llangadwaladr, Cybi of Llangybi and Padarn of Llanbadarn. Shadowy holy figures recorded in place names include Collen of Llangollen, Bride of Llansantffraid, Grwst of Llanrwst, Curig of Llangurig, Tydfil of Merthyr Tydfil and Melangell or Monacella of Pennant Melangell.

Brychan is another mysterious, perhaps mythical, holy figure. He, it is said, was the head of a veritable dynasty of saints which included many of his children who numbered variously from a dozen to more than sixty. These were said to have included Clether, Dwynwen, Morwenna, Nectan and Tydfil, and several of them settled in Devon and Cornwall where the villages of St Clether and St Endellion record the names of two of them. Another little-known saint is Brynach to whom Nevern Church, near the coast of Dyfed, is dedicated. While many tales told of Celtic saints involve decapitation, martyrdom and murder, Nevern preserves one of the most endearing stories which encrust the Christian faith.

As the long, dark nights of winter waned the people of Nevern would await the coming of their harbinger of spring. On Brynach's feast day in early April they would gather near the churchyard cross of their patron saint and scan the southern sky. Year after year the sighting of a distant dot would send a ripple of excitement through the assembly. On the same day each year a cuckoo would wheel down from the Preseli Hills and swoop into the churchyard. There the cuckoo, the first of its kind to arrive from the heat of Africa, would hover above the upturned faces and land on Brynach's Cross amid the yew trees to announce the arrival of spring. But one year the people of Nevern gazed into an empty sky. Something was wrong. Morning became afternoon and no bird came gliding and diving from the south. Men and women shuffled, the agitated priest became tense, his eyes revealing his anxiety – Mass could not begin until Brynach's messenger had delivered its song.

The shadows of evening lengthened, the air grew chill, the assembly began to drift away, heads hung in disappointment. Then someone cried, "There! There!" Low and slow, against the darkening mass of Mynydd Preseli, a bird was making its laboured approach. Sometimes it fell towards the ground to vanish from sight before its wings bore it up again. Over the river and up to the churchyard came a cuckoo in staggering flight. Wings motionless, the bird dropped onto the disc-cross atop the saint's stone. The parishioners edged forward to the carved curvilinear decorative panels. Its breast pumping with exhaustion, the cuckoo raised its head in echoing song. Again the first cuckoo to be heard in all Pembrokeshire had announced the start of spring from Brynach's Cross in Nevern churchyard. As the pople gave praise in their church by candlelight, the harbinger's cuckoo-song and heart-beat died.

Brynach's Cross at Nevern is one of the finest Celtic crosses in Wales, dating from around the 10th century. Overlooking the medieval church, which has two stones with Latin and Ogham inscriptions from the early centuries of British Christianity are the remains of a motte and bailey castle built by Norman invaders. Contrary to oaths sworn on holy relics,

Rhys ap Gruffydd (Lord Rhys) ejected his young son-in-law, William FitzMartin, from the stronghold and gave it to his wily son Gruffydd, but father and sons fell out, Rhys was beaten in battle – a divine punishment for breaking his promises – and locked up in Nevern Castle. Also in the churchyard are old yew trees, the subject of folkloric speculation, because red sap 'bleeds' for the woes of Wales, and not far away Nevern has a rock carved with a pilgrims' cross to mark the way for travellers seeking the cathedral shrine of St David. The area of the Preseli Hills is rich in prehistoric structures which include Bedd yr Afanc (the monster's grave), the Iron Age hillfort of Foel Drygarn topped by three ancient cairns, the stone circle of Gors Fawr, and Pentre Ifan cromlech.

The most famous shrine and holy well of medieval Wales was that of St Winefride (Gwenfrewi) whose life was the subject of a bloody and violent legend. This well-connected seventh century young lady – her father was a prince and her uncle a saint – was the object of unwanted attention by a young nobleman called Caradog. When his attempted seduction of Winefride failed, he flew into a violent range and she girded up her skirts and ran, hoping to reach the sanctuary of uncle Beuno's church. The rejected suitor gave chase down the hill, caught up with his prey, took out his sword and sliced off her head. Retribution was swift; the earth opened up and Caradog's maiden-chasing days were ended forever, while a spring gushed forth where Winefride's head had landed. Some say her head then rolled on down the hill, went through an open church door and came to rest at the feet of her uncle who was conducting a service at the time. Be that as it may, Beuno picked up his niece's head, replaced it on her shoulders and so restored her to life. Some say that Winefride lived out her life as a nun at Holywell, the place of her miraculous recovery; others tell that she entered a remote valley convent at Gwytherin whence her relics were stolen away by the English who wanted to entice more of the pilgrim trade to Shrewsbury Abbey.

Holywell's popularity as a place of pilgrimage blossomed in the late medieval period and Henry V visited Winefride's Well in the year after his victory at Agincourt. Lady Margaret Beaufort, matriarch of the Tudor dynasty, was a prominent patron, paying for a new chapel to be built over the well. Shrine and cult survived the Reformation and James II who had no male heir after 15 years of marriage to Mary of Modena, came seeking the saint's blessing in 1686. Two years later James was given the good news of the birth of a son and the bad news of an invasion which chased him and his heir out of the kingdom.

Winefride's shrine was administered by Cistercian monks from nearby Basingwerk Abbey, founded by a 12th century Norman Earl of Chester. A miraculous tale of a saint's intervention concerns a young nobleman of the family of Hugh Lupus (the Wolf), the hated and cruel Earl of Chester, who decided to make a pilgrimage to Holywell's shrine. In a time when Welsh and Norman warriors were fighting for control of north Wales it was a perilous undertaking, and the earl's Welsh foes got wind of the trip and planned to capture and ransom the pilgrim.

Fortunately the young nobleman escaped the ambush and gained sanctuary in Basingwerk Abbey which was promptly besieged by the kidnappers. The pious visitor went to the abbey church and sought the intervention of Werburga, a saint whose relics resided in a shrine at Chester. Suddenly a great wind arose and, to the astonishment of monks and besiegers, a huge sandbar bridged the Dee estuary, and across it from the Wirral, with pennons flying from their lances and sun glinting on armour, the earl's army came galloping to the rescue. A more likely site for such an escapade would have been Basingwerk Castle near Bagilt, then a motte and bailey outpost of which there are scanty remains.

The monks did very well out of the pilgrim trade at Holywell where the water of Winefride's Well was said to be particularly beneficial for skin disorders. But in 1917 the water supply was interrupted by local mining operations and the well ran dry until a new source was found. Now the water runs again into a star-shaped basin in a chamber decorated with scenes from Winefride's life beneath the restored Tudor chapel. Another curious tale connected with the shrine is that its water can reveal guilt as happened in the case of a goat thief. The suspect denied that he had stolen and eaten the animal so he was brought to the well to put the matter to the test. Although the omens indicated him guilty of the felony he continued to deny all knowledge of the matter whereupon the argument was resolved by all the parties plainly hearing the stolen creature's bleats issuing from the man's belly.

Decapitation was a fate shared by many saints. According to legend Winefride's uncle Beuno came upon the scene of a murder in his travels. Some years before a peasant with ambition had wormed his way into royal favour and married a princess. Although he had achieved a comfortable station in life, the man was nagged by the fear that his low-born origin would be discovered by his wife so his drastic solution was to cut off her head. A spring bubbled out of the ground where the innocent lady's head lay and then Beuno came along and put the head back on her shoulders to restore her to life. Arild, who lived near the Severn, had her head cut off when she refused to lie with a lustful lord. Tydfil, one of Brychan's daughters, was killed by pagans and the site of her grave became Merthyr Tydfil. Another of Brychan's murdered kin was Clydog who was a victim of jealousy. A young lady had eyes for only Clydog and this enraged another of her suitors who killed Clydog while they were hunting in the Black Mountains. As with Walstan of Norfolk, the oxen pulling the hearse indicated the burial site by refusing to go beyond the Monnow river ford below Merlin's Mountain. The place where they buried Clydog and built a church in his memory is called Clodock. A few miles to the north-west is the isolated circular churchyard of Merthyr Cynog, burial place of a hermit whose head was chopped off by pagans while he was at prayer. Cynog recovered his head from a well which then dried up and walked to his lonely hermitage for burial.

Endellion, another of Brychan's daughters, went to Cornwall where she was sustained by the milk of a single cow which wandered off to pastures new, angering the landowner upon whose meadows it trespassed. He killed the cow causing Endellion to go hungry. News of the lady's loss reached her godfather and the butcher was done to death, but the forgiving holy virgin restored him to life. Brychan's eldest son, Nectan, made his way to Devon to settle down as a hermit-cowherd. When his animals were rustled he tracked down the culprits and preached to them about their wicked ways. His message was lost on the gang and they chopped off his head whereupon, to their amazement, he picked it up and walked back to his hermitage to expire beside a holy well. Decuman, a Welsh monk, endured a similar fate in Somerset; he toted his head back to his birthplace near Pembroke. Justinian, a hermit on Ramsey Island, was plagued by devils who appeared in various forms. They chopped off his head, the usual well appeared, and Justinian marched across the Sound with his head under his arm to the place that bears his name and where a chapel, now ruinous, was dedicated to his memory. Another version is that he was the victim of disciples who had no stomach for his rigorous and austere regime of prayer and toil. Collen, the patron of Llangollen, is said to have rid that area of a man-eating giantess who was depopulating the region. After a prolonged battle which put a stop to her anti-social behaviour, Collen washed away the stains of the ogress's blood in the waters of his well.

Teilo, a sixth century monk, bishop and saint of south Wales, left a crop of tales about his life and work. The name of the tiny village of Llantilio Crosseny (Teilo's church by Ynyr's cross), near Abergavenny, preserves a story from the days when pagan Saxons were raiding into Christian Wales. Ynyr, the chief of the district, sought the saint's help against the invaders and was told to set up a large wooden cross as a mark of his faith. Teilo prayed, Welsh swords and spears scattered the Saxons and the grateful Ynyr gave the saint land upon which to build a new church. The present building, medieval in origin, has many historical points of interest including a carved 'Green Man', a face with foliage issuing from its nose, a reminder of pre-Christian fertility beliefs. Another tale is that of Teilo's skull. Penally near Tenby claims to be the place of the saint's birth and death. On his deathbed, Teilo instructed a nun to carry his skull to a church he had founded near Maenclochog, and there it was to be used by those suffering from coughs and consumption as a cup from which to drink water from his holy well. Later it was said that the cure would only be effective if the water was offered to the sufferer in thc skull by its hereditary keeper who was a member of a local family. Three places, Penally, Llandeilo and Llandaff, claimed to have Teilo's relics and this was explained by a miracle which occurred when the saint died. The monks faced a quandary; they did not know which of the three places had the best claim to his remains so they prayed for guidance and then went to bed. The next day their problem was solved when they found three identical corpses. Oaths sworn at Teilo's shrines were considered to be particularly binding because those

*St Govan's Chapel tucked beneath coastal cliffs where,
long ago, a saint lived the life of a holy hermit.*

who broke their word could expect the saint's retributive intervention.

Dwynwen, another of Brychan's offspring, gave her name to Llanddwyn Island, Anglesey, and bequeathed a romantic cult in which she became the St Valentine of Wales. One version of her tale is that she fell madly in love with a prince in a rather one-sided affair, so much so that she prayed to be cured of her paining passion, a wish which was fulfilled when her lover was turned into a block of ice. Dwynwen considered this to be a decidedly extreme method of cooling male ardour and was granted three wishes. At her request the unfortunate man was defrosted, never again did she suffer the pangs of desire, and she asked that all true and faithful lovers should meet no impediment to their union. Her shrine achieved fame and prospered thanks to the offerings of those who came to have the fish and bubbling water of the well pronounce on the sincerity of their partner's protestations of undying love.

Another well where maidens could discover the truth of their suitor's intention was Ffynnon Gybi (St Cybi's well) at Llangybi, a well also good for warts and rheumatism. There they would cast a fine linen kerchief upon the waters and watch expectantly to see which way it floated – if it drifted north his words were false, but if it gravitated southward then his heart was true. In other places a feather or a snatch of wool from a hedge would do. At another of Cybi's wells, at Llangybi near Lampeter, sufferers of aches and pains would bathe in the well then pass the night under an ancient stone; if they slept recovery was assured. A similiar ritual had to be followed by cripples at Llangeler in the Teifi valley where, long ago, a collection of crutches accumulated from those who had slumbered soundly in the churchyard. Lurking in the depths of another of Cybi's wells was an eel which gave assurance of the treatment's success by corkscrewing its serpentine body around a leg – a heart-stopping experience for the unsuspecting.

Once a year the well of Caradog, a court minstrel turned monk, allowed young women to see the likeness of their future spouse in return for an offering of three bent pins. Another traditional rural method was for a girl to soak a petticoat in a saint's well and then dry it in front of the cottage fire when the rising steam would take the shape of her intended. If it failed to do so the maiden was doomed to spinsterhood. In some places there was a wedding day custom in which the newly-weds had a race to see who would 'wear the trousers'. Bride and groom sprinted from the church porch to the local saint's well in the traditional belief that the first to drink of its waters would hold the purse-strings and rule the household.

Beuno, the wandering monk and abbot, founded a monastery at Clynnog-fawr where his tomb and well acquired a reputation for healing. Some sought his blessing for their cattle, those afflicted with sore eyes would soothe their pain with a balm of powder scraped from the stonework mixed with well water, and sickly children bathed in the water and then spent a night on his tomb – if they slept recovery was guaranteed. Cybi set up his monastery in the old Roman fort at

Holyhead, and Tudwal had his chapel and hermitage on one of the little islands which bears his name off Abersoch before he departed for Brittany. Along the Lleyn road to Bardsey Island a troubled pilgrim could seek relief at the local holy wells for a variety of ills – warts, stomach ache and loose bowels, lameness, scabby skin and melancholia.

Bardsey Island (Ynys Enlli) was for many centuries a home of monks and a goal for pilgrims. Local fishermen would doff their hats as they sailed past 'the island of 20,000 saints'. The monastery was founded by Cadfan in the fifth century and three pilgrimages to Bardsey were the equivalent of one to Rome. The island is another of those places where the wizard Merlin is said to sleep after foolishly giving in to the wiles of a woman. Others say that at dawn, black-cowled spectral figures appear and raise a wailing chant as a warning of impending plague or violent storm. Among them, perhaps, is the ghost of Dyfrig (Dubricius) who retired to Bardsey as abbot and died there in the mid-sixth century. Geoffrey of Monmouth, a 12th century priest who lived much of his life in Oxford and recorded Merlin's prophecies and many other fanciful deeds and characters in his book 'The History of the Kings of Britain', said that it was Dyfrig who crowned the 15-year-old Arthur as King of the Britons. The relics of Dyfrig, who was so pious that he could cure anyone of anything, were removed to Llandaff in the 12th century in a bid to boost that place's depressed pilgrim trade and it was there that Geoffrey died in 1154.

Another scholarly churchman and a near contemporary of Geoffrey was Gerald of Wales (Giraldus Cambrensis) whose chronicles of curious events, scandals, characters and phenomena give a unique insight into life in 12th century Wales. Gerald had an unflattering 'dig' at Geoffrey's book, which he considered untrustworthy, by telling a tale about a soothsayer called Meilor who lived near Caerleon. One evening he had been enjoying himself in the arms of lovely girl when, suddenly, he found himself cuddling a hairy monster, a circumstance which, not surprisingly, addled his brain. Fortunately his sanity eventually returned but he was left with an ability to see and talk with demons who delighted in pointing out liars, insincere monks and untrue statements. When the little devils plagued him he drove them away by putting a copy of St John's Gospel on his knees, but when he replaced it with Geoffrey's 'Historia' back came the little devils to pester him more than ever.

Gerald was born in 1145, the youngest son of a Norman knight and a grandson of Gerald of Windsor, the constable of Pembroke Castle, and Nesta, a Welsh princess renowned for her beauty whose extensive list of lovers included Henry I. Gerald's ambition was to be Bishop of St David's (he wrote a book about David's life) but his Welsh blood was against him – the English kings would not consent to his nomination on political grounds – and despite hazardous journeys to Rome Gerald's expectations ended in disappointment. In 1188 he accompanied Baldwin, Archbishop of Canterbury, on a recruiting drive around wild Wales, their mission being to drum up support for the Third Crusade. It was a long and perilous journey in which they faced quicksands, dangerous river-crossings and the fear of attack and robbery. They set out from Hereford and made their way via Radnor and Brecon to Caerleon where, according to Geoffrey, King Arthur had held court and Guinevere became a nun, then along the south coast to St David's. The party then headed north to Caernarfon and Bangor, journeyed on to Chester and returned through the Marches to Hereford, a circular tour which took almost two months.

Gerald recorded the happenings and miracles which occurred along the way as well as tales of demonic spirits and curious customs. He spiced his book with anecdotes, some scandalous, about the princes, nobles, knights and monks through whose lands they travelled. Among the strange creatures he noted were a deer-cow (deer at the front and cow at the rear), one-eyed fish and eels, and beasts half monkey and half dog. He tells of faithful greyhounds guarding their masters' dead bodies, an eagle which waited to feed on post-battle corpses, and the castellan of Radnor Castle whose hounds went mad after he had irreverently turned Llanafan-fawr church into a dog kennel. The knight himself was struck blind and he ended his days when he got some friends to take him to Jerusalem, place him aboard a warhorse and point him at the enemy – a Saracen sword-swipe terminating his miserable existence.

Another knight, says Gerald, suffered labour pains for three years and eventually gave birth to a calf. In Pembroke Castle a man who moved a nest of new-born weasels – animals then considered to be venomous – saw the distraught mother attempt to avenge the theft of her young. She spat poison into a jug of milk intended for the man's young son but when her young were returned the forgiving weasel knocked the milk jug over so that the child would come to no harm. A man who lived near Nevern and dreamed of finding gold in St Brynach's well was not so lucky – as he groped for the treasure he was bitten on the hand by a lurking snake and died. Another resident of Cemais suffered a most bizarre end. He was Seisyll, an ill young man whose sick-bed was invaded by an army of toads. No matter how many were killed they kept on coming. The patient was hoisted to the top of a tree but the toads climbed up after him and made a meal of poor Seisyll of whom only a skeleton remained. Other 'wonders' recorded by Gerald included a battlefield near Cardigan where an army numbering two of Gerald's uncles among its ranks had been put to flight was marked by an old burial mound which changed shape and broke swords; Pembrokeshire poltergeists and a rock on Barry Island which transmitted the sounds of a subterranean blacksmithy.

During an overnight stop at Nefyn, Gerald had a stroke of luck – he discovered Merlin Silvester's long-lost book of prophecies (Gerald, who wrote accounts of the 'discovery' of King Arthur's and Queen Guinevere's tomb at Glastonbury, believed there had been two Merlins). Flemish colonists in Wales had their own way of prophesying – they studied the shoulder bones of sheep to find out what fate had in store. One man whose wife was pregnant by their grandson tricked his unfaithful spouse into revealing her shameful secret by having her 'read' a bone which she thought belonged to someone else. Ram-bone reading endured as a widespread superstition with those who knew the 'art' being consulted about propitious days to begin journeys, the outcome of pregnancy or whether a maiden should marry. During their journey Gerald and Archbishop Baldwin did plenty of preaching – at Haverfordwest an old woman's blindness was cured when she applied to her eyes the turf on which the primate had stood, and a Cardigan housewife who held on to her husband's belt to stop him 'taking the cross' was punished by unwittingly smothering her young son in her sleep. Three days later her husband joined the ranks of the Crusaders. Among other miracles Gerald recorded were the cases of a boy who tried to steal birds from Llanfaes Church near Brecon and was stuck to a stone, he being released after three days of prayers with the stone preserving his fingerprints; a priest who tried to blow a blast on St Patrick's Horn was struck dumb and lost his memory; and the healing power of St Curig's gold and silver encrusted crosier in St Harmon's Church which cured warts and boils for a penny. At Glascwm a handbell belonging to St David was looted by the soldiers of Rhayader Castle, an act which resulted in the whole town being burnt down.

Gerald bequeathed a literary portrait of the Welsh people of his time. The men were agile, moustachioed battle-lovers who usually fought as barefoot infantry with little armour; they considered it a disgrace to die in bed (families slept together in a hard communal bed) and they took great pride in fine horses and weapons. They were notably hospitable and generous, they loved music and singing, ate masses of meat but little bread, and unlike the English they were assiduous in the care of their teeth, cleaning them with twigs and wool. Less endearing traits included their treachery and untrustworthiness, their murderous feuding and love of plunder which caused them to break their oaths and promises.

Caldy Island, once a haunt of pirates, still has a community of monks. Long ago it was called Ynys Pyr in honour of its abbot who some said came to a disreputable end when he got drunk and fell down the well. He was succeeded by Samson who left in disgust at the brothers' unholy behaviour. Bishop Samson was aptly named because several places claim to have massive stones which he tossed about. Llanbadarn Fawr, named after Padarn (Paternus), and forerunner of Aberystwyth until English invaders built a new castle and borough nearer the sea, has two Celtic crosses as evidence of Samson's strength. He was threshing three miles away at Maes-bangor (monastery field) when the smaller stone, the flail-head, flew off and landed in the churchyard. In frustration, the short-tempered saint hurled the other, the handle of the defective tool, after it. Among the prehistoric structures of Dyfed is Carreg Samson near Abercastle, a burial chamber with capstone on three supports once hidden beneath a mound of earth. In the next bay beyond Mynydd Morfa a poor, hard-working fisherman gave assistance to an injured mermaid. He lived out his life in modest comfort because never again did he come home but with his little boat filled with the finest and tastiest fish. Abbot Pyr had lands at Manorbier (Maenor Pyr) described by Gerald as the finest spot in all Wales, although he admits his bias because he was born there; and across the bay is St Govan's Head, a place with many a strange tale to tell.

Hard by the sea beneath craggy cliffs is the spot where Govan, a sixth century Irish hermit, lived his final years in religious isolation. Steps cut into the cliff descend to a tiny chapel – a traditional puzzle is to count the steps going down and then see if you get the same answer on the way up. Govan's well, now dry, was good for bad eyesight and lame limbs, particularly when the water was applied from a sea-shell. A 19th century traveller noted that cripples, some from the remotest parts of Wales, bathed in the water and left their crutches on the altar as votive offerings. A cleft in the rock inside the chapel is said to be the opening which miraculously appeared when pirates invaded Govan's seclusion; he climbed in and the rock closed behind him. It is also a place where wishes are sometimes granted – if you can turn around in it. The empty bellcote, so it is said, testifies to another of Govan's encounters with pirates who stole his silver bell. The raiders thought they had got their hands on some easy loot but as they sailed away the bell dropped through the bottom of the hull and sank the ship which took them with it. Angels recovered the precious bell and encased it in a rock for future safety. Some say that old Govan was really King Arthur's loyal knight, Gawain, who lived in pious retirement here. A nearby rocky ravine known as Huntsman's Leap got its name from a daring horseman who jumped it and then died of fright when he realised what he had done.

A man who gained a bloodless victory over his foes with a shout was Germanus, a Gallic bishop who came to Britain (quelling a storm on the way) to chase out heresy. In 429 he was made general of a British army when heathen Picts and Saxons were on the rampage. He set up camp near Mold, baptised his troops in the river Alyn and then prepared an ambush. On his order, his men shouted "Alleluia!" three times and the enemy, thinking the sky was falling on them, took to their heels. This famous victory at Maes Garmon (Germanus' field) is marked by an obelisk set up in 1736. Not so fortunate were the hundreds of monks who joined an army against Ethelfrith, a pagan king of Northumbria. They came from the most famous monastery in the land at Bangor-is-y-coed, once home of Pelagius, author of the heresy which Germanus quashed. The Battle of Chester in 607, won by the Northumbrians who 'slew a countless number of Welsh', was interpreted as divine judgement for defiance of Augustine, the first Archbishop of Canterbury. Bede claimed that 1,200 monks were killed and that their monastery was destroyed; 50 tonsured survivors ran all the way to Bardsey Island. The Anglo-Saxon Chronicle puts the number of 'priest' casualties at 200. A few years earlier Ernin had survived his traumatic experience and found sanctuary on the island as a monk. He was a son of Helig whose lands were drowned by the sea.

Tewdric was another saint killed in battle by heathen Saxons. He gave up his crown in old age to become a hermit, but he answered a call to arms and led the warriors of Glamorgan to a victory in which he suffered a mortal wound. More than a thousand years later in the 17th century his skeleton with smashed skull was found at Mathern Church. Another hermit of south Wales was Issui who lived a lonely life in the Black Mountains. One night he gave food and shelter to a lost traveller and the ungrateful stranger murdered the holy man. Issui's hermitage at Petrisio became a shrine, and legend tells that the building of the church was financed by a hatful of gold left by a grateful pilgrim who was overjoyed at being cured of leprosy.

Among the Berwyn hills of Powys, where waterfall and streams give birth to the river Tanat, another remote and tiny church marks the shrine of a little known saint who is the subject of a gentle and winsome tale. She was Melangell, or Monacella, a runaway Irish princess who had fled to this delightful spot to escape a forced marriage. Brochwel, Prince of Powys, was hunting in the hills one day when the sound of horns and the cry of hounds started a hare. The chase was on. The hare darted in a grove from which the baying hounds retreated and scattered, and when a hunter put horn to mouth to recall the dogs it stuck to his lips. Brochwel advanced to investigate and found Monacella kneeling in prayer with the hare peeping out from the folds of her robe. The prince gave the lady land in Pennant where she formed a community of nuns, and in respect for her memory no hares (Melangell's lambs) were hunted in the parish for centuries. Her tale is told in carvings in the 12th century church which still has the saint's medieval shrine, a unique survival from that period. The church also has two old effigies, one of the saint herself with two hares peeking out from her dress at the waist, and the other of a 14th century warrior-prince sheathing his sword.

Another church of ancient ancestry stands high and solitary above the Conwy valley and, according to tradition, it lost a princess from its congregation because the climb was too steep. Llanrhychwyn Church is a mile south of Trefriw where Llywelyn ap Iorwerth (Llywelyn the Great) often held court, and on Sundays he and his wife Joan had to make the wearing climb to the little church which, some say, is the oldest in Wales. Eventually, to silence his wife's complaints, Llywelyn built a new and easily accessible church at Trefriw. The north aisle of Rhychwyn's simple church, where candles are still the only source of light when it gets dark, was added by Maredydd ap Ieuan, an ancestor of the powerful Wynn family of Gwydir. Maredydd, who died in 1525, was the master of Dolwyddelan Castle and the builder of a new church in that village. There the brass likeness of him kneeling in his armour is unique, it is the only military figure among fewer than 20 memorial brasses in all Wales.

According to Sir John Wynne, Maredydd, who fathered 26 children, also had problems when he wanted to go to church on Sundays which was why he demolished the old building 'which stood in a thickett' and built the new one 'in a plaine, stronger and greater than it was before'.

The church of Llandewi Brefi built on the mound which rose beneath St David's feet while he preached.

Maredydd explained that 'the country was wild, and he might be oppressed by his enemies on the sudden in that woody country, it therefore stood him in a policy to have divers places of retreat. Certain it was that he durst not go to church on a Sunday from his house (it was about a mile south of the church) but he must leave the same guarded with men, and have the doors sure barred and bolted, and a watchman to stand at the Carreg-big during divine service, being a rock whence he might see both the church and the house, and raise the cry if the house was assaulted. He durst not, although he was guarded with twenty tall archers, make known when he went to church or elsewhere, or go or come the same way through the woods and narrow places lest he should be laid for.'

Tales of the deeds of David (Dewi), patron saint of Wales, are legion. Strict and austere, it is said he founded many monasteries, including Glastonbury. The old monastery at St David's (it vies with St Asaph in claiming to be the smallest cathedral city in the realm) was sacked by Vikings and rebuilt in the 12th century. Following David's canonisation in 1120 his shrine became an important pilgrimage centre, two journeys there counting as one to Rome. His mother, Non, is said to have been a princess or a nun – her tomb is in Brittany – and Geoffrey of Monmouth claimed that David was King's Arthur's uncle. A chapel, now a ruin, and a well good for poor eyes dedicated to Non stood above St Non's Bay and around the headland of Trwyncynddeiriog (Madness Point) is Porthclais, the traditional site of her son's baptism. Miracles began from the moment of David's birth, an event signalled by a terrible thunderstorm. A blind man had his sight restored when splashed with baptismal water, springs and wells appeared where he healed the sick and lame, and others burst forth when he struck the ground with his staff, prayed for water to slake his thirst or where his tears hit the earth. Apart from their medicinal value, it was said that they never ran dry in summer or froze in winter. At Llanddewi-Brefi the ground rose up under his feet to lift him above the crowd when he was preaching and now a church dedicated to him stands on the spot.

The many wells attributed to David reflect his abstinence – he would drink only water – and one is said to mark the spot where he restored to life a poor widow's son. Cenydd, who like other babes of Welsh fable such as the bard Taliesin, is said to have begun life by being set adrift in a wicker basket, was healed of his deformity by David but demanded to be restored to his natural state. Legend claims that Clegyr-Boia, a small prehistoric hillfort near St David's, was the camp of a heathen robber chieftain, Boia, whose wife was particularly malevolent towards David. To tempt his monks from their vows of chastity she ordered the tribe's seven most alluring women to go naked into the monastery, but thanks to David's example celibacy prevailed. When one of her daughter's became a convert she lured the maiden into the woods on the pretext of gathering nuts and berries, then, as they rested with girl's head on her lap, she cut the virgin's throat. Where the blood flowed a spring of pure water spouted to wash away the stain but not the memory of the murder. Some wells were said to be the lair of serpents, eels and even dragons, and the behaviour of fish in the waters was interpreted as omens, good or ill. Bathers hung their old bandages on nearby trees or thorn bushes in the belief that as they decayed in the wind the wound, wart or sore would heal. Garments placed on the water predicted the outcome of treatment – floating was a sign of assured recovery, sinking foretold failure or death. Thieves could be discovered by floating an object which sank when the culprit's name was spoken; murderers revealed by the water turning red; bewitched artefacts 'cleansed' of curses by holy well water; sins and Sunday toil were punished by springs drying-up. Tales arose of wells being haunted by the restless spirits of unavenged murder victims, love-lorn suicides, or killers who had tipped the corpse down the well.

Failing sight, rheumatism, rickets, scrofula, scurvy, scabs and a multitude of skin disorders were common among the ailments which people believed could be alleviated by well water. Women could be cured of sore breasts and sterility, men of baldness, impotence and the pox. Some wells had specific days and times, often dawn or sunset on a saint's day, when the treatment was considered to be most effective.

Superstitious rituals became linked with some wells and springs. Often, where a standing stone or cromlech stood nearby, it too became part of the healing rite. Some megaliths were supposed to have their own magic powers and to sleep on them through a night offered the gift of poesy at the risk of madness or death. Suppliants had to follow the prescribed ritual with care – at one wart-curing centre they were warned that deviation carried the risk of 'inheriting' the warts lost by previous customers. Tegla's well at Llandegla was noted for its treatment of epilepsy. The afflicted had to make three evening circuits of church and well while saying prayers, then sleep in the church using a Bible as a pillow, in the company of a caged chicken. The next day the patient blew into the chicken's mouth and released it; if the bird died it was a signal that the cure had been effected.

Of the cursing wells that with the most dreaded reputation was Ffynnon Elian at Llanelian-yn-Rhos. One 19th century guardian of the well was jailed for carrying on the notorious but lucrative tradition. The victim's name would be scratched on a slate or written on a piece of paper which was dropped into the well and then, to the accompaniment of recitations and water-throwing ceremony, the curse would be pronounced. The prestige of the well was such that it attracted the patronage of hundreds each year. Jealous rivals, envious competitors, rejected suitors, deceived maidens, and wives suspicious of their husbands' fidelity were high among the clientele. Farmers whose crops failed or beasts died, those afflicted with sudden aches and pains, the plain unlucky, anyone who suspected malevolent victimisation could pay the keeper to consult his register to see whether they were among the jinxed. If so, for a fee the curse could be lifted by having their name retrieved from the well and expunged from the book of the accursed.

Gelert's Grave — the memorial to a Prince's faithful hound which saved a royal babe from a hungry wolf.

Castles, kings, princes and poets; passions, paramours and phantoms

Ruin seize thee, ruthless King!
Confusion on thy banner wait,
Tho' fanned by Conquest's crimson wing
They mock the air with idle state.
Helm nor hauberk's twisted mail,
Nor even thy virtues, Tyrant, shall avail
To save thy secret soul from nightly fears,
From Cambria's curse, from Cambria's tears!

With these words the poet Thomas Gray imagined a bard 'robed in the sable garb of woe' calling curses down upon the head of Edward I as the conquering king rode through Snowdonia in 1283. After celebrating his successful campaign of annexation with a tournament at Nefyn, Edward and his architect, James of St George, busied themselves with the building of mighty castles to control the region. Artisans and labourers from almost every shire of his kingdom were drafted into Gwynedd to build new stone castles at Conwy, Caernarfon, Harlech and later Beaumaris. Barons richly rewarded with Welsh lands raised castles for themselves at Denbigh, Chirk, Ruthin and Holt; the strongholds at Flint, Hawarden and Rhuddlan were completed and the small Welsh castles of Criccieth, Dolwyddelan and Bere were repaired. Wales was a land thick with castles from the Marches to the coasts – Oswestry, Montgomery, Dinas Bran, and Wigmore; Cardiff, Caerphilly, Carmarthen, Cardigan, Carew and Carreg Cennan; Builth, Brecon and Aberystwyth; Kidwelly, Tenby, Pembroke and Abergavenny; and scores more. The relics of ancient conflicts abound – Celtic hillforts, Roman legionary camps, motte and bailey castles and strongholds of stone – and the stories of these and the men and women who lived in and fought for them have been woven into the fabric of folklore.

Probably the best known of all Welsh 'legends' is the story of a prince, a greyhound, a wolf and a babe. Every year thousands of tourists visit the memorial to a mythical greyhound at Beddgelert (Gelert's grave) – their pilgrimages being the product of a brilliantly imaginative and enduring tourist-trade hype. In the concocted legend, Gelert, was the favourite hunting dog of Llywelyn the Great, Prince of Gwynedd. But one day the loyal hound, a gift from the prince's father-in-law, King John, failed to appear for the hunt and when Llywelyn returned home he found –

The hound all o'er was smeared with gore,
His lips, his fangs, ran blood . . .
Blood, blood he found on every side,
But nowhere found his child.

Believing Gelert had eaten his son, Llywelyn plunged his sword into the dog whose dying cry awoke the unscathed child hidden beneath tumbled bedding. The truth became evident when Llywelyn found the bloody carcase of a wolf –

> *His gallant hound the wolf had slain,*
> *To save Llewelyn's heir.*

> *And now a gallant tomb they raise,*
> *With costly scuplture decked;*
> *And marbles storied with his praise*
> *Poor Gelert's bones protect.*

> *And till great Snowdon's rocks grow old,*
> *And cease the storm to brave,*
> *The consecrated spot shall hold*
> *The name of 'Gelert's grave'.*

It was not a famous Prince of Gwynedd who raised Gelert's 'tomb', the cairn was the later work of David Pritchard, keeper of the village inn in the late 18th century, and his friends, and the popular verses were penned by Regency socialite William Spencer.

Llywelyn ap Iorwerth, the supposed slayer of Gelert, was the most powerful of the medieval Welsh princes. Born in Dolwyddelan Castle, he sided with the barons against King John and was a signatory of Magna Carta in which John promised to respect Welsh rights and hand over Llywelyn's hostage son. He was also the man who came closest to uniting the country under a single ruler. Gerald of Wales, who believed the English fought for power and profit and the Welsh for liberty, considered that Wales could never be subdued if its rulers ceased their feuding and combined under one prince. Llywelyn had deposed his uncle to become master of Gwynedd and he married Joan, King John's illegitimate daughter, whose affair with a Marcher baron ended with her lover hanging from a rope's end. William de Braose had been taken captive in a skirmish near Kerry and a ransom and marriage between his daughter and Llywelyn's son secured his release. In 1230 de Braose returned to the Welsh prince's court at Aber where Llywelyn's castle guarded the route across the Lavan Sands and there he continued his liaison with Joan. Their secret, however, was discovered and, according to tradition, when Joan said she would happily give up everything to see her lover, a window was thrown open to reveal de Braose dangling in the courtyard. Joan died in 1237 and was buried at Llanfaes, Anglesey, in a friary founded to her memory by Llywelyn who ended his days in the precincts of Aberconwy monastery. Their rest was disturbed by military expediency. The monks of Aberconwy were shifted to Maenan (taking their benefactor's coffin with them) by Edward I who wanted to build Conwy Castle, and a few years later the king did the same to the people of Llanfaes when he needed stone for his castle at Beaumaris. Joan's stone coffin, used as a horse-trough after the Reformation, is now in Beaumaris Church and Llywelyn's is at Llanrwst.

The name de Braose had been made hateful to the Welsh many years before the events at Aber when another William de Braose, a grandfather of Joan's lover, treacherously massacred Welsh nobles in Abergavenny Castle. This infamous act had its roots in the decades of conflict between the Welsh princes and the land-grabbing, castle-building Normans. Bernard de Neufmarche, lord of Brecon, had seized estates in the Marches in the late 11th century and he married Nesta, a lady of royal Welsh descent and evil repute. She liked to pass her nights in the arms of a handsome knight, a faithless activity of which her son, Mahel, thoroughly disapproved. One night Mahel intercepted his mother's lover on his return from the lady's bedchamber, gave him a beating which left him scarred and sent him packing. Nesta, filled with vengeful fury, huried off to the court of King Henry I where she swore that Mahel had not been born in wedlock but was the result of another illicit affair. The 'bastard' Mahel was disinherited and Bernard's lands passed by the marriage of daughter Sybil, whom Nesta acknowledged as having been fathered by her husband, to Milo FitzWalter, later Earl of Hereford.

Milo and Sybil had numerous offspring and when Milo was killed by an ill-directed arrow while hunting in 1143 there were five sons lined up to keep the estates in the family. But fate, which Gerald of Wales saw as retribution for grandmother Nesta's wickedness, decreed that they should all come to untimely ends. One by one the brothers died or were killed, and the last of them, another Mahel, made his earthly exit after a brief tenure of the domain in 1175 when he was hit on the head by a stone which fell off the top of Bronllys Castle. This last of Earl Milo's male line expired believing he had suffered divine retribution for hounding the Bishop of St David's out of the diocese. So once more the lordship passed by a daughter to a new family, that of William de Braose, 'the ogre of Abergavenny'. Seeking to avenge the killing of one of Milo's sons, de Braose invited Welsh chieftains to a feast at Abergavenny and murdered them all. A few years later the sons and grandsons of the victims stormed the castle in a dawn raid. Destiny had a cruel end in store for de Braose. King John feared the Marcher baron was getting too big for his boots and de Braose ended his days in exiled beggary. His wife, whose scandalmongering tongue was largely responsible for the family's fall, went into folkore with a frightening reputation for witchcraft and she died a hideous death by starvation with her son, whom she had part eaten, in a dungeon of Windsor Castle.

In Tudor times a bishop of St David's tried to take out of circulation a lady with a reputation for witchcraft and generous favours by locking her up in Llawhaden Castle but she was rescued by Thomas Wyriott who came galloping to the rescue at the head of his troops. They say that the lady had her revenge by sticking pins into a model of the bishop who relented and allowed her to return home on condition that her behaviour showed a marked moral improvement. The poet-warrior Huw Llwyd was said to have known something of the mysterious science of wizardry; he lived near Ffestiniog and his 'pulpit' is a rock near Rhaeadr Cynfal. On his way home from a war against the Spanish he lodged at a lonely inn run by a couple of kindly looking sisters, but during the night he was awakened by a couple of black cats clawing at his clothes. Grabbing his sword, Huw gave one feline a smack across the paw – next day he noticed one of the beldams had a bandaged hand and realised that the landladies were using the black arts as well as the tariff to empty travellers' pockets.

The Normans held their Welsh land by the power of their swords and Milo, Earl of Hereford, found that for some of God's creatures it was no substitute for inherited right. One day he and Payne FitzJohn, lord of Ewias, were riding with Gruffydd ap Rhys ap Tewdwr near Llangorse Lake, a lake so productive that it was said to be two-thirds water and one-third fish. Milo mocked Gruffydd's claim to royal lineage and teasingly reminded the Welshman of a belief that only the true ruler could make the birds of the lake greet him with song. Gruffydd challenged the Normans to test the legend and the birds steadfastly ignored their shouted commands. Then Gruffydd got off his horse, walked to the lakeside and thousands of wintering wildfowl immediately raised their voices and beat the water with their wings in acclamation. Gerald of Wales recorded the story and said that Llangorse Lake sometimes turned bright green and bloody red, and that in winter it moaned and groaned; he explained the latter phenomenon by saying it was probably the ice cracking.

A sister of 'rightful ruler' Gruffydd was another Welsh princess named Nesta. The most renowned beauty of her time, she gained a reputation very different from that of her Brecon namesake. She had several children by her lovers, among whom she counted Henry I and Marcher lords, and it was due to the amorous side of this lady's nature that her grandson, Gerald of Wales, enjoyed such a convenient network of relationships with many noble families, Welsh and Anglo-Norman. Nesta's husband was Gerald of Windsor, the commander of Pembroke Castle who built an outpost at Carew on land which was part of his wife's dowry. Owain, a prince of Powys, was one man smitten with a passion for Nesta and he put a blight on Gerald's Christmas festivities by kidnapping the desirable lady (who seems to have had no objection to the abduction) and carrying her off to a love-nest near Llangollen. King Henry raged and threatened reprisals, Nesta was restored to her husband and Owain was later killed in a skirmish with Gerald's troops.

Henry FitzHenry, Nesta's son by the king, was among the force which ravaged Anglesey in 1157 after Henry II had narrowly escaped ambush near Flint. The English looted shrines (including Llandyfrydog where Hugh of Montgomery's dogs had gone mad) which greatly angered the Welsh saints in heaven, so wrote Gerald of Wales. Fired by vengeance and with St Tyfrydog on their side, the ill-armed and outnumbered

Gronw Tudur at Penmynydd – his alabaster tomb was chipped to provide eye-wash for the dim sighted.

locals killed many of the invaders, FitzHenry among them. Robert FitzStephen, Nesta's son by the castellan of Cardigan, was sorely wounded but managed to escape to the ships. The Welsh princes combined against Henry II in 1165 when an English army, leaving burned churches in their wake, advanced on Corwen and pitched their tents on Berwyn Mountain. Unseasonal August storms and rain from the heavens made life miserable for the English and they had to tramp home hungry; Henry vented his rage by blinding and mutilating more than 20 noble hostages including sons of the Welsh princes. Henry had fared better two years earlier when he had marched against Rhys ap Gruffydd. Merlin had predicted that if a strong, freckle-faced man crossed the old ford of Rhyd Pencarn (near Newport,Gwent) at the head of an invading army the Welsh were sure to be beaten. Old locals gathered near the disused ford to see where the king would cross the river; Henry approached the usual crossing place but his horse shied when trumpeters on the far bank blasted out a fanfare and carried him full tilt through the water at the old ford. Rhys soon surrendered to big, befreckled Henry who, some say, became a clear complexioned king when he paused to wash the sweat off his brow.

Ifor ap Meurig, known as Ifor Bach because of his short stature, had better reward when he boldly kidnapped an earl from Cardiff Castle. William, Earl of Gloucester, had robbed him of some land so Ifor climbed into the well-manned castle, abducted the erring earl, as well as his wife and son and carried them off to the forest. Ifor let them go when his estate was restored plus some extra for his trouble. Some years earlier, in 1098, Gerald of Windsor had cunningly ended a siege of Pembroke Castle. With the garrison weakened by desertions and the food almost gone, Gerald cut up four hogs and showered the besiegers with pork chops; he also wrote a letter, which he knew would fall into enemy hands, saying he would have no need of help for several months. It was all too much for the Welsh who dispiritedly packed up and went home.

The amorous Nesta had a sister-in-law with a martial streak. In 1136 Gwenllian overconfidently led an army against Kidwelly, even taking her young sons along to witness female generalship, but the rugged Normans upset the script by choppping off the mother Amazon's head and chasing her troops from the battlefield which from thenceforth was called Maes Gwenllian. Her headless spectre is said to haunt the castle while another feminine spook which puts in an occasional appearance is another lovely Nesta who lived in Kidwelly Castle long ago. She jumped into a river after the body of her beloved Norman knight, Walter Mansel, who had been foully murdered as they were about to meet on a bridge. Norman knight Payne de Tuberville was luckier. When Robert Fitz-Hamon, builder of Cardiff's first castle, handed out the spoils of conquest in Glamorgan there was nothing for Payne who was told to go and win his own domain. Tradition has it that he came to Coity, the stronghold of a local chieftain, who, holding a sword in one hand and an attractive daughter in the other, offered him the choice of combat or marriage. Payne elected the latter and so won himself a bride and a castle.

Castel Dinas Bran, perched on a hilltop above Llangollen, was once the home of celebrated beauty, Myfanwy Fechan, whose charms inspired bards to verse, but, as one of them admitted, getting her to smile was even harder than the climb up the mountain. By the Tudor age the castle within prehistoric defences on Dinas Bran (City of the raven) was a ruin and the breeding home of a fierce eagle which attacked anyone who went near its nest. The castle had been built by Gruffydd ap Madog as a retreat from the hostility of his countrymen caused by his marriage to an English baron's daughter. At his death, legend says, English allies were entrusted with the custody of his young sons who conveniently and suspiciously drowned under Holt Bridge. It was beside the Dee at Holt that the Earl of Surrey, who had been given Dinas Bran as the spoils of war, preferred to build a new castle, while Roger Mortimer raised a new stronghold at Chirk on land which had once been Gruffydd's.

The most remarkable bard of Welsh legend was Taliesin. He was the son of the witch Ceridwen, wife of Tegid, lord of Penllyn whose city lies beneath Bala Lake (Llyn Tegid). The infant Taliesin was found floating in a basket by Elphin whose Cantref y Gwaelod homeland was lost to the sea. Elphin had been looking for salmon and did not consider a babe to be much of a consolation prize until the infant began singing verses. When Taliesin entered his teens, Elphin went off to Deganwy Castle to spend Christmas with his uncle, King Maelgwyn Gwynedd, who unfestively chained him up when Elphin boasted of knowing a bard better than the king's two dozen fawning praise-singers. Taliesin rescued his foster-father by singing up a mighty storm which almost frightened the life out of Maelgwyn, and humiliating the court bards who suddenly found that they could utter only infantile finger-on-lip noises. Bedd Taliesin, an ancient burial chamber near Tal-y-Bont, is the traditional tomb of the mystical bard who, some say, was also a knight of the Round Table. An historical Taliesin was chief bard to King Urien of Rheged.

The first eisteddfod for bards and harpists is said to have taken place at Caerwys in 1100 at the summons of Gruffydd ap Cynan, the half Viking Prince of Gwynedd. The first recorded competition for poets and musicians was a Christmas contest in 1176 at Cardigan Castle when Rhys ap Gruffydd handed out prizes. An eisteddfod at Caerwys in 1568 by order of Elizabeth I was designed to weed out the vagabonds who travelled the land earning a living by indifferent talent. It had been the duty of the bards to gather and be the guardians of the 'three memorials of Britain' which listed the deeds of kings, the genealogies of the nobility and preserved the ancient tongue. Two famous medieval Welsh poets got into trouble over ladies – Dafydd Nanmor, who lived near Pont Aberglaslyn, had to pack his bags when he addressed verses to Gwen, a lady whose husband failed to appreciate the sentiments; and Dafydd ap Gwilym ('the Horace of Wales' according to George Borrow) who sent scores of poems to Morvydd, an Anglesey 'princess' with whom he eloped. They were tracked down

Roch Castle where a snake-haunted warrior met his prophesied doom from the fangs of the lurking serpent.

and handsome Dafydd's love was made to marry a rich old man.

Two ladies who 'having been crossed in love, foreswore all dreams of matrimony in the heyday of youth, beauty and fashion, and selected this charming spot (Llangollen) for the repose of their now time-honoured virginity' were Eleanor Butler and Sarah Ponsonby, the two eccentric 'Ladies of Llangollen'. For half a century after 1780 the pair of cultured Irish bluestockings lived with their maid at Plas Newydd, a much altered mansion with black-and-white timber façade, where they entertained the foremost politicians and literary giants of their day. Katheryn Tudor of Berain near Llannefydd had no shortage of suitors and had two proposals of marriage on the day of her first husband's funeral. As she came out of church, Morris Wynne of Gwydir asked to be her second spouse but he was disappointed because she had already accepted Sir Richard Clough who had escorted her in. She did, however, console him by saying that if she lived to bury Sir Richard then Wynne assuredly would be husband number three. Katheryn then made certain that there was yet another husand-in-waiting by pledging her troth to Edward Thelwall that he would be number three if death removed Wynne from the queue. Indeed she did marry Clough, Wynne and Thelwall in their turn and died in 1591 in her fifties. A portrait of her in younger days has her with left hand on a skull – folklore tittle-tattle said she did away with her spouses and buried them in the garden – and a locket at her breast which was said to hold the hair of Sir Richard, her favourite of the four. Katheryn's marriages into so many powerful families caused her to be called the 'mother of Wales' and Thomas Salusbury, a son by her first husband, got involved in a plot to free Mary Queen of Scots and was executed.

A royal favourite with Henry II long ago was 'Fair Rosamund' who was born in her father's border castle at Clifford; but she was not such a favourite with Queen Eleanor. Tradition has it that Henry ensconced his secret love in a comfortable retreat surrounded by a maze at Woodstock but sharp-eyed Eleanor spotted a silken thread caught on his spur and followed it with fatal result for poor Rosie.

> But nothing could this furious queen therewith appeased bee;
> The cup of deadlye poyson stronge, as she knelt on her knee,
> She gave this comelye dame to drinke; who took it in her hand,
> And from her bended knee arose, and on her feet did stand,
> And casting up her eyes to heaven, she did for more calle;
> And drinking up the poyson stronge, her life she lost withalle.

A more lurid version is that shameless Rosie was stripped, dumped in a tub of ice-water between two braziers and while one wicked hag beat her another planted venomous toads on her breasts. Lucy Walter, the first of Charles II's list of paramours, was born in Roch Castle above St Bride's Bay. During the Commonwealth when Cromwell's troops were busy blowing great holes in Welsh castles to stop the Royalist gentry from turning them into bastions, Lucy gave comfort to the then prince in exile and bore him a son. Lucy died young in a foreign land before Charles was called home to his patrimony and their son, James, Duke of Monmouth, lost his head after failing to topple his uncle James II. They say Adam de la Roche built his castle on a rocky hill at Roch because he had a dread of snakes; but castle walls could not save him from his fate – a servant brought in a bundle of firewood wherein lurked unseen a viper which emerged during the night to fulfill a witch's warning.

Another tale of venomous doom comes from Penmynydd on Anglesey where church effigies of ancestors of Tudor kings and queens have been chipped by folk who thought alabaster flakes from the tomb made a curative potion for dimming eyes. It had been foretold that the only heir of a noble family would be slain by a dragon which wandered the marshy banks of Afon Braint. For years the lad was kept out of harm's way and great was the rejoicing when word came that the beast was dead. The youth, freed at last to wander where he would, hastened to see the corpse of the monster which had been the bane of his young life and the supposed end of his fears made him careless – he disdainfully kicked the lifeless skull, stabbed his toe on a venomous fang and expired. A dragon which landed on the ruined castle at Newcastle Emlyn caused consternation at the village fair. The fearsome flying serpent had a stony and seemingly bullet-proof skin but a sharpshooter spotted that its belly-button was unprotected, hit the mark with a musket-ball and sent the beast crashing into the Teifi whose water its blood turned red.

A dragon-slayer before the days of gunpowder was St Llwchaiarn who built his church at Llanmerewig in Powys. The church was transformed in eccentric style by a 19th century rector who later moved across the border to Llanyblodwel, Shropshire, where he again indulged his singular and amateur architectural skill with a bulging stone spire. Powys has several folktales of demons being miniaturised to convenient size by wizardry so that they could be trapped and rendered harmless in a bottle or box. One tradition tells of a spirit which caused havoc in the shape of a huge bull and which could only be reduced by a parson uttering holy texts and prayers. Unfortunately the beast reassumed inflated proportions during the night when the weary cleric's invocations were halted by his candle burning out. The parson started again at dawn with renewed vigour, slowly belittled the demon to the size of a cat and then, like John Shorn who besides relieving gout and toothache 'conjured the Devil into a boot', the miniscule bull was pushed into a buskin and buried in a church porch so that the 'weight of the parish' could trample over it twice a week.

A tunnel from Carreg Cennan Castle, a cliff-top fortress traditionally founded by one of King's Arthur's knights, leads to a cavern where whispered wishes were granted and the water was good for deafness. At Oystermouth, where lived Dr Thomas Bowdler, the man who removed words of impropriety and so 'bowdlerized' Shakespeare's works, local lore claimed that a stone in a dungeon had been known to grant the desires of young men and women who had walked backwards around it nine times. Orville Owen, a doctor from Detroit, believed Shakespeare's works had come from the pen of Sir Francis Bacon whom he considered to be the son of Queen Elizabeth I. By 'deciphering' texts Owen concluded that a hoard of Bacon's manuscripts was buried near Chepstow Castle but all he dug up was some old iron. Chepstow's old castle was besieged twice during the Civil War. In 1648 it was held for the Royalist cause by Sir Nicholas Kemoys who was killed in the assault – they say the boat he kept ready for escape was cut adrift by a Roundhead soldier who swam across the river with a knife between his teeth. Henry Marten, the convinced Republican whose wench-chasing angered Puritan colleagues, was locked up in the castle for the last 20 years of his life for having signed the warrant which sent Charles I to the scaffold. Marten, who had dressed up a friend in the 'toys and trifles' of the coronation regalia of kings, was buried in Chepstow Church in 1680 having had plenty of time to compose his epitaph which advises 'care then not how you end, but how you spend your days'.

Montgomery (Trefaldwyn or Baldwin's town as it was known to the Welsh from the name of a Norman commander of its castle) is a quiet village with a history punctuated by violence. Its 13th century castle on a steep-sided narrow ridge has been a ruin since the Commonwealth when Lord Edward Herbert handed it over to Parliamentary forces on condition that his beloved library in a new house, which he had built in the castle precinct, would be undamaged. In his younger days Lord Herbert claimed that his figure attracted the attention of several queens, old and unwed Elizabeth I among them, as well as numerous ladies of the court who, so he boasted, wore his picture next to their hearts to the anger of their husbands. In Montgomery Church is the huge emblazoned tomb of Lord Herbert's parents who are shown in lifelike repose above father Richard's shrouded cadaver. It is, however, a grave near the churchyard's north gate which is the subject of a famous tale.

John Davies was a man with a mysterious past – 'a melancholy, grief-haunted man' was how a parson described him – but he was a good farm-manager. In 1819 he became the steward of widow Morris' run-down farm near Chirbury and his hard work soon changed the fortunes of the widow and her daughter Jane. Davies' success roused the jealousy of Thomas Pearce who had wanted to buy the farm, and Robert Parker who nurtured hopes of marrying Jane. With the passage of time Davies and the widow's daughter became friendly, even affectionate towards each other in a warming relationship which threatened to end Parker's and Pearce's plans forever. A conspiracy was hatched to get rid of Davies by having him convicted of a crime and transported to the other side of the world. One dark November night Davies was walking home from Welshpool fair when he was waylaid by the conspirators who forced him to return to that town where they accused him of robbery. Instead of a crime carrying a sentence of transportation, Davies was tried on a charge of highway robbery with violence which carried the death penalty. Davies was found guilty and when sentence of death was pronounced he again swore his innocence of the charge, "I protest most solemnly, before that God in whose presence I must shortly appear, I am entirely guiltless of the crime for which I am about to suffer. I do not say that I am an innocent man, I have committed a crime, but it is known only to my Creator and myself." He then told the court, "I venture to assert that if I am innocent of the crime for which I suffer, the grass, for one generation at least, will not cover my grave."

On the day of Davies' execution in 1821 the sky became overcast as the bell tolled the signal – "no sooner had he placed his foot upon the scaffold than a fearful darkness spread around; and the moment the fatal bolt was withdrawn, the lightnings flashed with terrific vividness, the thunders rolled in awful majesty, until the town hill seemed shaken to its base; the rain poured down in torrents; the multitude dispersed horror-stricken and appalled, some crying out – The end of all things is come!" Of the other characters widow Morris and her daughter left the area, Parker was killed in a blasting accident and Pearce 'wasted away from the earth'. Three decades later a clergyman recorded that no grass had grown on the plot and that attempts to cover 'the Robber's Grave' with grass using fresh soil, new seed or fresh turves had all proved vain.

Montgomery Castle had been one of the castles held by the Mortimers, a powerful Marcher family who came close to gaining the throne. In 1327 Roger Mortimer was involved in killing a king in a most hideous manner in Berkeley Castle on the English side of the Severn. The victim was Edward II who, as an infant at Caernarfon in 1284, had been presented to Welsh nobles as 'a prince born in Wales who could speak no English'. Edward of Caernarfon was the first son of a king of England to be proclaimed Prince of Wales, a title granted at the discretion of the sovereign, not claimed by right by an heir to the throne. Edward II was the antithesis of his masculine, dominating and decisive father, and in 1326 an alliance of the lovers Mortimer and Isabella, Edward's wife, the 'she-wolf of France', deposed the foolish and weak king whose advancement of favourites had angered many barons and made Mortimer a bitter enemy. Edward took shelter in Caerphilly Castle which sustained a long siege by the queen's forces, but he was captured at Neath Abbey, betrayed by a monk, while trying to escape to Ireland. A few months later he was done to death and Mortimer and Isabella ruled in the name of her young son. In 1330 Edward III asserted his rights – he locked up his mother in a draughty Norfolk castle while Mortimer, who had been seized at Nottingham by a raiding party which got into the castle by a secret passage known as Mortimer's Hole, was executed at Tyburn.

During the six centuries from the Norman invasion to the Civil War the castles of Wales played a periodically violent and often dominating role in the life of the principality. Norman kings and adventurers built them as centres of power in a contested land, Welsh princes raised them to defend their homeland, and in later wars they were besieged and defended by Owain Glyndwr's armies, Yorkist and Lancastrian partisans during the Wars of the Roses, and Royalists and Roundheads of the Civil War. Many were allowed to decay; some were converted to the less

Raglan Castle, scene of a Civil War siege in 1646.
When the castle surrendered it was made indefensible.

martial and more elegant lifestyle of post-Restoration gentry; others became prisons for debtors and felons. Many of the deeds and characters from those far-off centuries entered the folklore of the land. Travelling through old Radnorshire in the early 18th century, Daniel Defoe noted that 'stories of Vortigern and Roger of Mortimer are in every old woman's mouth' – perhaps one of the tales he heard was how an earlier Roger Mortimer had waived his hat on the top of a hill as the signal for the rescue of the future Edward I from rebel barons at Hereford, and then galloped away with the prince to the safety of Wigmore Castle.

William the Conqueror's creation of the Norman Marcher earldoms of Chester, Shrewsbury and Hereford brought new and aggressive foes to the eastern border of Wales. These were warrior barons with almost regal powers who could build castles without royal consent, grant charters and wage their own 'private wars' of expansion. They founded castles to defend their lands against Welsh attack and encourage trade and economic development, although some, like Caus, Cefnllys, Kilpeck, New Radnor and Richard's Castle, failed to prosper, as did Llywelyn ap Gruffydd's desperate bid to check the central advance with a castle and town at Dolforwyn. Hugh Lupus advanced along the north coast building castles at Rhuddlan, Deganwy and Caernarfon but Princes of Gwynedd ejected the Normans and built their own border castles such as Ewloe and Tomen-y-Rhodwydd. The earls of Shrewsbury advanced up the Severn Valley and the conquest of Brycheiniog, Gwent and Glamorgan was marked by dozens of motte and bailey strongholds. The march up the west coast was checked and repulsed in the 12th century by Rhys ap Gruffydd (the Lord Rhys) who held castles at Cardigan, Dynevor, Drysllwyn and Llandovery.

England's baronial wars against King John and Henry III were exploited by Llywelyn the Great (died 1240) and his grandson, Llywelyn ap Gruffydd who was recognised as Prince of Wales in the Treaty of Montgomery in 1267. The days of Welsh independence, however, were drawing to a close. In 1277 Edward I invaded Gwynedd and stripped the Welsh prince of much of his hard-won power, and another war, sparked off by the sacking of Hawarden Castle in 1282, completed the conquest. Edward built boroughs defended by strong stone castles at Caernarfon, Conwy, Harlech and, after a revolt, at Beaumaris; the captured Welsh-built castles of Gwynedd had a less favourable future. Dolbadarn, where Llywelyn had locked up his rival brother Owain for 20 years, was abandoned; isolated Castell y Bere was rebuilt but soon deserted; and Criccieth (mound of the captives) was refurbished and occupied until its destruction by Owain Glyndwr's forces in 1404. Among the captives who had been held at Criccieth Castle was Gruffydd, Llywelyn the Last's father, who later broke his neck when a rope broke during an attempted escape from the Tower of London. A famous constable of Criccieth Castle was Sir Hywel ap Gruffydd, also known as Hywel y Bwyall (Hywel of the Battleaxe) who was knighted at the Battle of Poitiers where he was said to have captured the King of France by slicing off the head of that unlucky monarch's horse with a single blow.

Owain Glyndwr's bid for independence and the Wars of the Roses brought ruin to many areas of 15th century Wales. Castles were besieged, towns sacked and robbers roamed the land – Carreg Cennen Castle was pulled down in 1462 because it was a haunt of brigands. Harlech and Aberystwyth endured long sieges and Caernarfon's garrison of 30 men repulsed Owain and his French allies; Conwy was taken while its defenders were at their Good Friday prayers in the town church. In the south and along the Marches it was a similar story – Carmarthen, Cilgerran, Usk, Picton, Hay on Wye and others fell, Coity, Grosmont, Pembroke and Carreg Cennan were among those which held out.

In the dynastic struggles between Yorkists and Lancastrians many castles were the scenes of war again. Iron-willed Margaret of Anjou, Henry VI's queen, found safety at Harlech after an adventurous cross-country flight but Lord Herbert, the Yorkist Earl of Pemboke, won Wales from his adversary Jasper Tudor, the Lancastrian Earl of Pembroke. At Harlech, a place where chroniclers said 'a livid fire' came off the sea to burn homes, barns and haystacks, the name of Dafydd ap Ifan entered legend. His defence of the castle is said to have inspired the song 'Men of Harlech' and he boasted that having held a French castle for so long that all the old women of Wales spoke his name, he intended to hold Harlech until the old women of France spoke of his fame. Harlech was the last Lancastrian stronghold to surrender, capitulating after an eight-year siege to Lord Herbert who demanded that the gallant commander's life should be spared, if not, he said, Dafydd would be put back in the castle and the king could have someone else try to get him out again.

Harlech was also one of the last Royalist strongholds to hold out in the Civil War. The time-consuming business of reducing them one by one caused Parliament to order many old strongholds to be made untenable but, fortunately, in some cases the instruction was ignored. Harlech was attacked in 1646 by Colonel John Jones, Cromwell's brother-in-law, who was born in Cwm Nantcol a few miles to the east below the slopes of Foel Ddu. Jones was one of the 59 signatories of the death warrant which sent Charles I to the scaffold and one of the nine regicides to be hanged, drawn and quartered when the monarchy was restored in 1660. The bullying president of the court who pronounced the death sentence on the king, Henry Bradshaw of Presteigne, escaped the traitor's death. He had died a year before the restoration but like Cromwell, his body was dug up from its grave in Westminster Abbey, his corpse hung on Tyburn gallows and his skull stuck on a spike.

Conwy was held for the king by the quarrelsome Sir John Owen who surrendered after a long siege; he was taken to London, sentenced to death but reprieved, and his memorial is in Penmorfa Church. One of the best commanders of the Civil War in Wales was Rowland Laugharne who fought for both sides. One of the castles he took for Parliament was Carew, once the home of Sir John Perrot who some said was fathered by Henry VIII. Perrot was given the castle and high office by his alleged

Pont Einon, the old triple-arched bridge from which a waggoner gave the Devil a shove into Tregaron Bog.

half-sister, Mary I, but when his other assumed half-sister, Elizabeth I, was queen he was charged with treason and locked in the Tower of London where he died. Carew is haunted by the ghost of one of its owners who, legend claims, was slain by his agitated pet ape after his son had married below his station. Laugharne switched sides in 1648, was defeated at St Fagans and retreated into Pembroke Castle with the town's former pro-Parliament mayor, John Poyer, while Colonel Powell, another former Roundhead, held Tenby. The siege of Pembroke lasted seven weeks and ended when a traitor told Oliver Cromwell how to cut the water supply – information for which the man was rewarded with a noose, not the cash he had hoped for. Laugharne, Powell and Poyer were sentenced to death but drew lots for two reprieves marked 'life given by God'; Poyer was the unlucky one and was shot in Covent Garden. Raglan Castle was a centre of Royalist resistance and the home of the Marquis of Worcester, one of the richest men in the land. Parliament supporters who came looking for guns were forced into undignified retreat when the old aristocrat switched on his son's noisy inventions and told the intruders that the lions were loose. In 1646 the marquis, who was well into his 80s, surrendered Raglan after a siege of 11 weeks and his castle was made indefensible.

The border fortress built by the Mortimers at Chirk was seized in 1644 by Royalists and they were besieged by Sir Thomas Myddelton, the castle's owner who had no desire to batter his own home with artillery. Fifteen years later Sir Thomas joined a premature Royalist rising and his castle home was attacked by troops who had no scruples about smashing its walls with cannon-balls. The damage was made good later with cash from a grateful Charles II. Chirk had been bought by another Sir Thomas Myddelton (father of besieger and besieged Thomas) a rich merchant and Lord Mayor of London, and he is one of the 16 children shown on his father's brass in St Marcella's Church near Denbigh. Among the nine brothers was Sir Hugh Myddelton who spent much of his fortune building a new water supply for London – "in 1608 the dauntless Welshman stept forth and smote the rock: and on Michaelmas 1613 the waters flowed into the thirsting metropolis." His brother William, voyager and governor of Denbigh Castle, was one of the first men to startle Londoners by smoking tobacco in the street. Conwy Church has a memorial to a man who came from an even larger family – Nicholas Hookes was his father's 41st child and himself the begetter of 27.

Among other phantoms said to haunt old castle ruins are a monstrous, big-eyed dog at Laugharne; the 'white lady' who guards buried gold at Ogmore; huge ever-living eagles protecting a treasure chest hidden from the Normans under Castell Coch; and Penard Castle was, according to legend, buried by sand when its warrior lord chased away frolicking fairies. Quiet coastal coves are haunted by the spirits of smugglers and pirates, and a cave near Aberdaron has the spooky presence of a poor old lady who thought it was her lucky day when she found a chest of gold on the beach – instead it turned out to be a bad day for her because she became so engrossed in counting her new fortune that she forgot about the in-coming tide.

A Welshpool woman who earned her living by spinning had a rewarding encounter with a ghost in Powis Castle. The servants thought to have some spooky sport by lodging her overnight in a warm and cosily furnished but notoriously haunted room. The firmly religious lady had no fear of spirits, so when the wraith duly drifted in and took up its pose she asked what it wanted (it was one of those polite ghosts which would speak only when spoken to). The spectre told her to pick up her candle and follow to another chamber where it revealed a hidden casket which, the phantom said, was to be despatched to the Earl of Powis in London. "Do this and I will trouble the castle no more," were the ghost's last words before vanishing. So pleased was the earl with the revealed box and its contents that the spinning lady lived out her days amply provided for. Loyalty to the Stuarts cost the Herberts of Powis Castle many years in exile. The castle was battered during the Civil War and when James II was deposed the Herberts followed him into exile, Lady Herbert smuggling out the infant Prince of Wales who grew up to be the 'Old Pretender'. Winifred, a daughter of the Powis Castle family of Jacobites, married Lord Nithsdale who was condemned to death for his part in the 1715 rising. When her pleas for pardon were rejected, Lady Nithsdale and her maid, Grace Evans, visited the Scottish lord in the Tower of London, dressed him in female garb and he walked out of his prison and escaped to exile in Rome. Winifred rewarded her loyal maid for her part in the daring exploit with the gift of a cottage home near Welshpool Church.

A dashing hero of a century later was Henry Paget, Earl of Uxbridge and Marquis of Anglesey. His bronze statue stands atop a column, one of the tallest structures on Anglesey, which was raised to mark his martial exploits against the French. He commanded the cavalry at Waterloo where a cannon-ball narrowly missed the Duke of Wellington and smashed his right leg. "By God! I've lost my leg!" exclaimed Paget who received a brusque reply from the Duke. Relations between the two commanders had soured in 1809 when Paget left his wife and family and eloped with Wellington's sister-in-law, Lady Charlotte Wellesley, a mother of four children. One consequence of the scandal was a duel between Paget and his new love's brother on Wimbledon Common in which the eloper refused to fire. Paget's Anglesey mansion home of Plas Newydd gives views across the Menai Strait towards the mountains of Snowdonia. Sir Thomas Picton who was born at Poyston, was killed leading his infantry division at Waterloo when a bullet through his top hat toppled him from his horse. A soldier and his horse who both survived bloody battles in the Crimea were Viscount Tredegar and 'Sir Briggs'. When the old warhorse died at Tredegar Park near Newport a monument was erected to the trusty charger which had carried its master safely through the Charge of the Light Brigade.

A less durable home than Tredegar House or Plas Newydd once stood in Lampeter; it was destroyed by fire after being cursed by a priest. The daughter of the house, the fair Elen, fell in love with a parson's son from Llandovery. Elen's four brothers did not approve of the affair and angrily abused the suitor who died of his injuries. The parson's vengeful execration on the household was, they say, powerfully implemented – the mansion burned down (as did another built with its stones), Elen died of a broken heart and the wicked quartet all came to a premature end.

Three times a week Rhys drove his waggon from Tregaron to Aberystwyth and back again. So regular and punctual was Rhys that people set their timepieces by him as he unhurriedly passed by puffing smoke from an old pipe. One cold and clear December night a cloaked and cowled figure emerged out of the shadows near Castell Flemish and jumped up onto the seat beside him. "Where are you from?" said Rhys pulling the pipe from his mouth. "A warmer place than this," replied the stranger. "Where are you going?" asked Rhys. There was a pause, then in a sinister tone came the answer, "Back where it is too hot for frost and snow – and you're coming too!" Rhys put the pipe back between his teeth, whipped the horses into an unaccustomed canter and, as they crossed the middle span of Pont Einon, he booted the passenger into the Teifi. That was the only time Rhys got back to Tregaron early and as he reined in his horses a thick, vaporous fog came rolling down the valley.

In the 19th century bands of curiously clad riders appeared on Welsh roads to the distress of the authorities. They were 'Rebecca and her daughters', men dressed in female garb who destroyed turnpike tollgates and tollhouses in violent protest against road charges. The 'Rebeccas' took their name from a verse in Genesis 24, "And they blessed Rebekah, and said unto her, Thou art our sister, be thou the mother of thousands of millions, and let thy seed possess the gate of those which hate them." The campaign forced the removal of many of the detested tollgates.

'Corpse candles' and the 'cyhirraeth' are the most blood-chilling sight and sound to be encountered in Wales and both are infallible forewarnings of death. The phantom procession of 'corpse candles' appears out of the gloom of evening and traces the route to the graveyard which the doomed person's corpse will soon follow. Fairies also foretell a mortal's death by marching with a black-veiled bier towards a churchyard. A priest who saw such a funeral party nearing his church believed they were mourners bringing the shrouded body of a parishioner whom he knew had been ill. But the moment he put his hand on the bier all vanished and he was left holding a horse's skull. The wailing 'cyhirraeth' is 'the king of terrors'. The invisible spirit's moan "begins strong and louder than a sick man can make, the second cry is lower but no less doleful, rather more so; the third yet lower and soft, like the groaning of a sick man, almost spent and dying; so that a person well remembering the voice, and coming to the sick man's bed who is to die, shall hear his groans exactly alike, which is an amazing evidence of the spirit's foreknowledge. Sometimes when it cries very loud it bears a resemblance of one crying who is troubled with a stitch."

A pitiful, wailing lament haunts the hills near Vortigern's retreat of

Nant Gwrtheyrn. Long ago the quarry village of Porth y Nant was the home of a young couple whose hopes for happiness seemed about to be fulfilled when their wedding day dawned. It was traditional for the bride-to-be to feign reluctance by hiding and then to be found and escorted to church by the bachelors of the community. But the maiden Maria was never seen again and the inconsolable bridegroom became a distraught searcher of lonely places. Many years passed and a violent storm cracked open an old hollow oak to reveal a skeleton in a wedding gown. Now their unquiet spirits prowl the hills in an endless search for each other.

Other spectral omens of misfortune which fill their beholders with fear and foreboding are insubstantial, foggy female forms. These devilish apparitions habitually lurk in lonely lanes or near crossroads and they delight in stalking travellers who, if they are wise, will elude pursuit by crossing a river or stream – water is certain to halt the phantom which can then only shriek in useless frustration. Some spooks are the spirits of men and women, murder victims, robbers and misers who have departed from this world leaving unfinished business; folklore says that they appear only between midnight and cock-crow, but never on Christmas Eve. A grocer's wife was entrusted with her dying mother-in-law's savings and told to share the cash with the rest of the family. The old lady's ghost came back to haunt the wife who failed to do as instructed and she was terrified into obedience by nightly visitations and a flight over the church steeple.

Phantom boats foretelling the death of sailors have been heard on Milford Haven; the spirits of church robbers transformed into fiendish dogs and demons have waylaid travellers (these restless spectres can be 'released' if the wayfarer has the courage to follow the ghost and restore the looted treasure to the church); and in mines a harmless race of little people known as 'knockers' have been heard boring and blasting underground.

A traditional game which required plenty of spirit from contestants because it was painful to play was 'cnappan'. Rival teams, sometimes hundreds strong, barefoot and stripped to the waist – shirts were soon torn to shreds and hair and beards 'trimmed' – battled for a wooden ball boiled in tallow. The game would range for miles with the teams trying to throw and carry the ball towards their own parish. "You shall see gamesters return home from this play with broken heads, black faces, bruised bodies and lame legs; yet merrily jesting at their harms, and all this in good mirth without grudge or hatred." An old notice in the church porch at Llanvair Discoed warned against other dangers risked by the participants of such pastimes –

Who ever hear on Sonday
Will practis Playing at ball
It may be before Monday
The Devil will have you all.